IMAGES
*of America*

SOUTHERN CALIFORNIA
FUNNY CARS

IMAGES
*of America*

# SOUTHERN CALIFORNIA
# FUNNY CARS

Steve Reyes

ARCADIA
PUBLISHING

Copyright © 2023 by Steve Reyes
ISBN 978-1-4671-0972-7

Published by Arcadia Publishing
Charleston, South Carolina

Printed in the United States of America

Library of Congress Control Number: 2022951071

For all general information, please contact Arcadia Publishing:
Telephone 843-853-2070
Fax 843-853-0044
E-mail sales@arcadiapublishing.com
For customer service and orders:
Toll-Free 1-888-313-2665

Visit us on the Internet at www.arcadiapublishing.com

*This book is dedicated to all the drag racing photographers
that have given this sport the attention it deserved.*

# CONTENTS

# ACKNOWLEDGMENTS

I would like to give thanks to Greg Sharp, Lou Hart, Bob "Stat Guy" Frey, Jamie Jackson, and Richard Shute of Auto Imagery for sharing images and stats. All photographs in the book are by Steve Reyes unless otherwise noted.

# INTRODUCTION

Southern California (SoCal) was the birthplace of the sport of drag racing, which was beginning to achieve new heights in popularity. With the help of Hollywood and the movie *Bikini Beach*, the kings of the quarter mile, the top fuel dragsters, had been played out on movie screens nationwide. The organized sport of drag racing was only 11 years old with the founding of the National Hot Rod Association by Wally Parks.

Parks is a natural leader and organizer who in 1951 founded the National Hot Rod Association (NHRA), and then two years later, the NHRA had its first organized event in Santa Ana, California. In Southern California, it was surf, sand, Hollywood, orange trees, and hot rods. The top fuel dragster became king of the quarter mile when the NHRA lifted its ban on nitromethane as a racing fuel (1957–1963). Now across drag strips in SoCal, the dragster racers were switching to nitro, and that meant faster racing.

Veteran dragster owner/driver Jack Chrisman was injured seriously while driving a dragster in May 1963. After six weeks in the hospital, he returned to his job at the Hi-Performance center at the Helen Sachs Lincoln-Mercury dealership in Downey, California. Fate stepped in when Fran Hernandez, the head of Mercury's racing program, gifted Chrisman with a brand-new stock Mercury Comet Cyclone. Hernandez wanted to get his longtime friend a car that Chrisman could play with at the races.

What Hernandez did not know was that Chrisman hated to shift gears in a car, any car, much less a race car. At first, Chrisman did not know what to do with his gift. He had his neighbor Bill Shrewsberry make a few passes in the car just to see what his new prize would do on the quarter mile. Meanwhile, in early 1964, Dodge debuted its Dodge Chargers race team, two matching Chargers with 480-cubic-inch supercharged engines on pump gas. Most drag fans considered these cars no more than gas coupes with modern-day bodies.

Chrisman asked himself, "Why not nitro?" So, with good friends Gene Mooneyham and Bill Stroppe, the first showroom-new stock-bodied Mercury Comet Cyclone was built that sported a blown nitro-burning 427-cubic-inch engine. Helen Sachs became Chrisman's main sponsor, with Sachs and Sons lettered on the doors. With paint and lettering hardly dry, Chrisman and his mini crew took the Comet to Northern California for testing at Fremont Drag Strip. One quarter-mile smoke-filled run and the car was ready for its NHRA debut at the largest race of the NHRA season, the US Nationals in Indianapolis, Indiana.

The standing-room-only crowd at the Nationals had an overwhelming response. Fans could not get enough of Jack Chrisman and his Comet's quarter-mile smoke-filled runs. But the NHRA did not know what to do with Chrisman and his Comet—there was no class for him to run in at the nationals. NHRA officials gathered and decided the Comet was a dragster, so the Comet was declared a class double-B fuel dragster. After the NHRA Nationals, the NHRA decided to start a new class just for the nitro-burning Comet and other super factory experimental or S/FX cars. Suddenly, across the United States, cars were popping up to race in the new S/FX class.

Thanks to Jack Chrisman, a new exciting class of race car was about to take over the sport of drag racing, the funny car class. Where did the term "funny car" come from? Well, Mercury's Fran Hernandez used the term to describe what Dodge, Ford, and Chevrolet racers had done to their factory-backed A/FX race cars. The racers had altered the wheelbases and modified the cars so much they all looked funny to Hernandez. He proclaimed that his Mercury racers were going to go out and beat those "funny cars," and the name stuck to this day.

# *One*

# VARIETY IS THE
# SPICE OF LIFE

Could it be that Gene Mooneyham and Al Sharp's 554 nitro-burning coupe was the first funny car? With driver Ron DeCicco, the blue 1934 Ford coupe topped 150 miles per hour in 1960. In 1963, the 392 blown Hemi-powered coupe cranked out an 8.96 at 170.77 miles per hour with "Jungle" Larry Faust at the controls. Many funny car purists believe that the 554 coupe was the first real funny car. (Courtesy of the Greg Sharp collection.)

Jack Chrisman's Sachs and Sons Mercury Comet was the first-ever showroom-new stock car to have a supercharged nitro-burning engine installed in its stock engine compartment. With Gene Mooneyham as his crew chief, the nitro-burning Comet astounded drag fans at the NHRA US Nationals in Indianapolis in 1964. With its quarter-mile smoke-filled runs, the car was considered one of the best shows in drag racing. Chrisman, Gene Mooneyham, and sponsor Helen Sachs, with the help of Mercury's Fran Hernandez, started a new era and class in the sport of drag racing on that long ago weekend. (Courtesy of the Greg Sharp collection.)

In 1965, Les Ritchey piloted a factory NHRA-approved A/FX Ford Mustang. The FX classes were considered the factory hot rods; A/FX, B/FX, and C/FX all raced under that banner. The big three auto makers followed the specs issued by the NHRA to race in those classes. The specs were steel-bodied cars with only two percent alterations allowed. The auto makers pretty much stuck to the rules, but their sponsored racers had other ideas. As pressure to win was laid upon the factory racers, cheating became more common in the A/FX class. The car's wheelbase was altered to transfer weight for better traction, and cars were stripped of excess weight to go faster and quicker. Mainly, this was happening in the Midwest and East to A/FX race cars. In Southern California, A/FX racing was a minority, and top fuel dragsters were kings of the quarter mile.

Garden Grove's Ray Alley had a different approach to drag racing in 1965. His "Big Al" was a one-of-a-kind funny car/race car. The car featured a one-piece fiberglass body that lifted off the heavy boxed-style chassis. But under that one-piece body was a P-51's 16-cylinder Allison aircraft engine. Of course, Alley's car was too heavy to compete, but he put on smoke-filled exhibition runs at SoCal and Northern California (NorCal) drag strips in 1965–1966.

"Dandy" Dick Landy did the funny car class no favors with his pathetic wheel stand shows. In Southern California, funny cars were considered a circus act and not real race cars. Landy's antics did not help much. A few Southern California track managers promoted funny car wheelie contests. They would match up Ford versus Chevy funny cars, and whoever did the longest wheelie won. It was no real side-by-side racing, just a sideshow for the fans in the stands.

With the success of Chrisman's Comet, Pasadena's Steve Bovan jumped onto the funny car bandwagon. About two months after Chrisman's debut, Bovan brought out his Blairs Speed Shop Chevrolet Nova. The 396 Chevy-powered Nova was supercharged and ran on 100 percent alcohol. His best time was 9.29 at 160 miles per hour. The car was one of the first US-touring funny cars from Southern California. Bovan raced everywhere in the East and Midwest putting on a great show for race fans. At the end of 1966, the car was sold to Ed Carter and Bob Little in NorCal. They revamped the Nova and renamed it the "Chevy II Heavy" and raced the 1967 and 1968 seasons in California and Washington State. (Photograph by Alan Earman, courtesy of the Lou Hart collection.)

Chrisman's Comet had a fresh look for 1965. For better traction and handling, the engine was set back and lowered. Fiberglass components replaced steel, and the car's color was now red. With all the changes the NHRA still had no official class for the Comet to run in except a fuel dragster class. The NHRA still thought the funny car was going to be a passing fad—how wrong would they be?

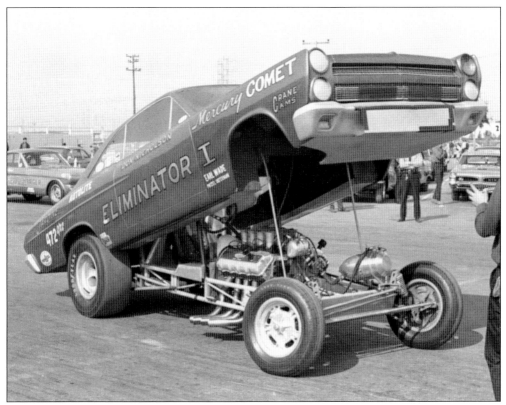

Fran Hernandez, the head of Mercury's racing program, was tired of all the cheating that was happening in the A/FX class. To address it, he ordered four Logghe Brothers tube chassis with four one-piece fiberglass Comet bodies. The complete turnkey race cars were given to Jack Chrisman, Don Nicholson, "Fast" Eddie Schartman, and the team of Kenz and Leslie. With that, Mercury declared war on all other car brands. Hernandez is credited with using the term "funny car" to describe what had become of the A/FX class and that Mercury had to go out and beat those funny cars—also known as cheating A/FX racers.

Circus time was over for Dick Landy in 1966. Wheelbase modifications, nitro, and injectors saw Landy get serious about racing. He even installed a supercharger for a brief time. But Landy, like Butch Leal and Don Nicholson, left the funny car class because of serious fire issues in funny car racing. Landy returned to the super stock classes, and in 1970, both he and Nicholson, along with Leal, became pro stock racers in the new NHRA pro stock class.

Bob Davis's "Jolly Green Giant" Chevrolet Impala was big, green, and loud. With a blown big block Chevrolet engine on a pinch of nitro, Davis and his Impala lumbered down the quarter mile. Since the Impala was too heavy, they ran it as an exhibition single-car show. Davis and his Impala were immensely popular at California drag strips in 1965 and 1966. The drag fans seemed to love this car because it was different, and they could relate to this family-style race car.

Who had the honor of being the first American Motors Corporation (AMC) funny car owner/driver? Well, that honor went to Preston Honea and his Bill Kraft AMC Marlin in 1965. Honea raced the Marlin from 1965 to 1966. The Marlin started out with a 327 Rambler engine, but with engine woes, it saw a switch to a Plymouth Hemi. The car did run a best of 9.83 at 135.33 miles per hour in mid-1966 with the Hemi.

In December 1966, the Fiberglass Trends Corvair funny car debuted at Irwindale, California. Rusty Delling was at the controls of the blue blown Corvair. The car soon vanished after its debut only to turn up with Bob Skukert racing the Corvair as a blown gas altered in his home state of Iowa.

In 1966, Jack Chrisman took charge of his all-new freebie Comet and, just like that, turned it into a Comet roadster. Chrisman's Comet roadster was soon the car to beat throughout the United States, as he seemed to be unbeatable. But all good things must come to an end, and it ended badly for Chrisman in New York. While appearing at a race at the New York National Speedway, the roadster caught fire and burned to the ground. Chrisman escaped, but the roadster was a charred pile of fiberglass and metal. This signaled the end of Chrisman's 1966 season, but never fear—Chrisman returned in 1967 with an all-new hard-top Comet to continue his winning ways for Mercury.

At the famed Smoker's March Meet in Bakersfield, California, Chrisman's new Comet and Al Vanderwoude, also known as "the Flying Dutchman," went head-to-head. The Smokers event had always been a top fuel dragsters–only event from its beginning in the 1950s. However, the new promoters from New York, Ed Eaton and Gil Kohn, were about to change things up. The first appearance of the funny cars at this event was in 1967. Although funny cars were classed as an exhibition, both Eaton and Kohn were impressed by the spectators' positive reaction to the exhibition, so funny cars were there to stay at the March meet.

One of the few Southern California Camaro-bodied funny cars was "the Bloomin Bullet" in 1967. Jerry Bloom owned the stock-looking Camaro, and Mark Bullet was its pilot. Together, Bloom and Bullet toured California, match racing and running a few open funny car shows in Southern California. The Camaro was injected and ran a fairly good load of nitro in the tank. Fiberglass doors, a trunk lid, and a fiberglass front clip helped shed some pounds off the stock-looking Camaro. The car ran the entire 1967 season, and then Mark Bullet left the team and went to drive for Tom Sturm and his "4 Chevy Lovers" Corvair.

At the 1966 Hot Rod Magazine Championships in Riverside, California, George Hurst debuted his twin-engine "Hurst Hairy Olds." "Gentleman" Joe Shubeck was at the controls of the twin-engine monster/smoke machine. Upon seeing the Hairy Olds run, top fuel racer John Smyser figured if Hurst could do it, so could he. Smyser acquired a slightly used Olds Tornado and turned it into his "Terrifying Tornado," another twin-engine quarter-mile monster, to make some of that funny car exhibition money. Smyser decided to drive it himself, which made every run more exciting for spectators. After a few bouts with Southern California guardrails, Smyser parked the twin-engine beast in late 1967; however, he returned to the top fuel class in 1969 with old friend "Hand Grenade" Harry Hibler as his driver.

One of the very early San Diego/El Cajon–area funny car racers was Randy Walls and his homebuilt 1965 Chevrolet Super Nova. Along with his wife, Cheri, and father-in-law, he toured California match racing and tried to race at every open show. His Nova was destroyed in a two-car crash at Irwindale in 1968. Frankie Pisano lost control of the Pisano Brothers Corvair at the finish line and hit Walls, sending both cars over the guardrail and destroying both race cars. Walls and Pisano were not injured in the spectacular accident. Both Pisano and Walls returned to Southern California funny car wars as soon as they could.

Southern California's Ronnie Runyan was one of the first funny car owners to put a nitro-burning supercharged engine in his 1963 Chevrolet Corvette funny car. Runyan took his gas coupe Corvette and turned it into the "Blue Hell" Corvette funny car. His Blue Hell could be a handful, but it did run well enough to compete with all the SoCal funny cars in 1967. He also raced in Northern California and did very well with his Corvette. Bigger things were in store for Ronnie and his brother Mike as they raced well into the 1980s.

World War II veteran Charlie Wilson and his "Vicious Vette" was a stepping stone for a couple of young unknown drivers in Southern California. Clyde Morgan began his driving career with Wilson's Corvette, and one of the future bright stars of the funny car class, Dale Pulde, got his start driving for Wilson. The candy-red Corvette was outdated, but the fans loved the car. The almost stock appearance was a big plus for Wilson and his Corvette in 1966–1967.

In 1967, the drag racing media billed Don Kirby's Fiberglass Trends Corvette as the world's fastest Corvette. The roadster-style Corvette had clocked several runs in the 200-mile-per-hour range with Pat Foster as the driver. Not only did Foster drive, he also built both top fuel and funny race cars. In his spare time, he also drove top fuel dragsters for a few different teams in SoCal. Foster drove for Kirby until mid-1969, and then Gary Gabelich took the reins of the newly sponsored Beach City Chevrolet Corvette.

The funny car craze was starting to get a grip on Southern California drag racers in 1967. Drag strip managers were now looking for cars to fill funny car events at their racetracks. Junior Brogdon had just the car for those promoters in his "Phony Pony" Mustang. Brogdon took a slightly used junior dragster chassis and made a "skinny" Mustang body to fit it. He then put a 289 Ford engine on nitro under the hood and declared it to be his Phony Pony funny car. Brogdon's race car was very funny and really appealed to kids because of its cartoon look. For the next two seasons, Brogdon ran two injected 289 engines on nitro and then switched to a blown nitro-burning 289 in his "Pony."

All new in 1967 was the Pontiac Firebird of Montrelli, Williams, and Barnett driven by Rusty Delling. This team disbanded shortly thereafter, and Pete Everett took ownership of the car, making it the "New Breed" Firebird running out of Everett's Chevron Station. Rusty Delling continued to be at the helm for Everett.

The honor of the first female nitro funny car driver went to SoCal's Paula Murphy. Paula's home-built Ford Mustang featured a Dave Zueschel 392 blown fuel-burning Hemi that was tuned by her crew chief, "Fat" Jack Bynum. The high-gear-only Mustang toured the United States in 1967. Many drag fans believed Murphy was the first woman to drive a nitro-powered drag car, but they would be wrong. Indiana-based Lynne Sturmer drove the "Bean Bandits" nitro-powered dragster in 1958 at US 30 Dragway in Gary, Indiana.

Gasper "Gas" Ronda was the dapper dance master of drag racing. The former Arthur Murray dance instructor left his mark on drag racing with his skill at driving stock, super stock, and A/FX race cars. In late 1966, Gas made the switch to a long-nose injected fuel-burning Ford Mustang sponsored by Russ Davis Ford in West Covina, California. Soon, Ronda became one of the most popular funny car drivers on the West Coast and capped off his 1967 season with a victory at the OCIR Manufacturers Race. His poppy-red Mustang outran all the blown funny cars to claim all the first-place monies. His Mustang ran a best of 7.90 at 184.04 miles per hour with only injectors on nitromethane.

Odd is the only way to describe Al Vanderwoude's "Flying Dutchman" Dodge Dart funny car. In the mid-1960s, Vanderwoude was racing a 1933 Willys gas coupe, but when the funny car class blossomed, he was there to join. In 1967, Vanderwoude entered the funny car world with a Ted Brown–built funny Dodge Dart. The topless creation was the longest funny car at the time at 132 inches long. It featured a blown 392 Hemi on nitro. Vanderwoude's Flying Dutchman Dart toured the United States in 1967, and in 1968, he changed over to a hardtop Dodge Charger funny car.

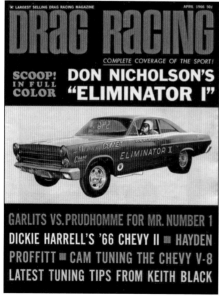

Out of the big four that Mercury sponsored in 1966, Don Nicholson proved to be the most popular of the racers. Nicholson's winning ways carried over to the new funny car class. His prior exploits in the A/FX class were well known to drag race fans across America. Early in 1966, Nicholson was rewarded with a cover and centerspread in *Drag Racing* magazine to the delight of the bigwigs at Mercury.

Race car header guru Doug Thorley replaced his injected fuel-burning Chevy Nova with an all-new Chevy Corvair for 1967. The car featured a big block Chevy engine on nitro and was built by SoCal's Pat Foster. Thorley and his mighty Corvair started 1967 by cranking out the first unofficial 200-mile-per-hour run for a funny car at Lions drag strip in Long Beach, California. Also in 1967, the Corvair ran a 7.69 elapsed time while winning the S/XS class at the NHRA US Nationals in Indianapolis, Indiana.

The funny car evolution was getting very funny at the start of 1967. The "Destroyer" was the funny jeep owned and driven by Gene Ciambella, and the 4 Chevy Lovers Corvair belonged to Tom Sturm. Ciambella traded in his gas coupe for the all-new Destroyer Jeep, while Sturm replaced his injected Chevelle with the all-new Corvair for 1967. Ciambella was only able to race his Destroyer Jeep for one season, because the NHRA banned Jeep-bodied funny cars, deeming them "too fast." Ciambella ran a new Firebird in 1968, but Sturm ran his Corvair in 1967–1968 before switching to a Challenger funny car in 1969.

A fitting example of recycling was Fred Goeske's purchase of a used Hemi 'Cuda. The rear-engine 'Cuda was the second of two that were built for Tom McEwen in 1965 and 1966. The first Hemi 'Cuda crashed when it flew at the Lions drag strip finish line. Sky pilot Tom McEwen was not injured in the rather hard landing. The second Hemi 'Cuda was never really raced and was just sitting when Goeske made an offer that Mopar could not refuse. Goeske debuted his new ride at Pomona in 1967 and raced the 'Cuda safely for the entire season.

The team of Stone, Woods, and Cook (SWC) were the stars of the gas coupe class in Southern California, and in 1967, it was time to go funny car racing. Their all-new Ford Mustang debuted at the NHRA Winternationals in Pomona, California. After a few practice runs, the team decided they were ready to go on a US tour. While racing at Alton, Illinois, the trio made the call to mount a rear spoiler on the trunk deck lid to stabilize the car at high speed. The spoiler was mounted backward, causing the front of the car to lift at the finish line. The ensuing crash destroyed the car and threw driver Doug Cook out of the car. Cook was badly injured but recovered; however, he never drove again. The team scrambled to get another SWC Mustang funny car back on tour to finish tour dates. Ron "Snag" O'Donnell drove the second SWC Mustang.

Wandering down from his native Canada, Dale Armstrong settled in Southern California. In 1967, along with Frank Pedregon, he raced the "Canuck" topless Chevy Nova funny car. The Nova was not a big threat in SoCal funny car racing, but both Armstrong and Pedregon took turns behind the wheel. They mainly raced at local funny car shows around SoCal. Dale gained much-needed driving experience behind the wheel of the Canuck, which came in handy for his future funny car rides.

The partnership of Ed Lenarth and Roger Wolford produced drag racing's first Jeep funny car, "the Secret Weapon," in late 1966. Their pairing was short-lived, but the Secret Weapon Jeep was very popular with the fans in SoCal. The duo had planned a US tour in 1967, but their parting stopped the tour. Wolford went and drove the "Mako Shark" Corvette funny car. Ed Lenarth still wanted to race a Jeep-style funny car, so he and Brian Chuchua put together the "Holy Toledo" Jeep funny car late in 1968.

Hardcastle and Akins's "Stinger II" was a one-of-a-kind funny car in 1967. Roger Hardcastle hailed from NorCal, and Pat Akins was from the San Diego area. The Stinger II was a kit car body from a do-it-yourself sports car kit with an Akins blown nitro-burning 392 Hemi powering it. SoCal's Gary Southern was at the controls. The Stinger II ran so well at local events that other funny car racers began to whine about the one-of-a-kind body on the car. They claimed it was an advantage over all the other funny cars in SoCal. The pressure was put on managers of local racetracks not to let the Stinger II race at local funny car shows. Finally, the managers buckled under the demands, and the Stinger II was banned from SoCal drag strips forever. It could run at fuel altered shows, but the fuel altered shows did not pay the same as funny car shows, so the Stinger was stripped and then sunk in a swamp in the San Diego area by Akins.

Veteran drag racer Hayden Proffitt went with a Chevrolet Corvair funny car for 1967. His Corvair featured an injected nitro-burning big block Chevy engine. His Corvair ran so well that the car would begin to lift at the finish line at speed. This could be a real problem and cause control issues that would end badly for Proffitt. He had a simple solution: cut the roof off and have a topless funny car. It worked. With no air collecting under the roof, the car was fine at high speeds, and Proffitt was happy.

Having sold his Nova in late 1966, Steve Bovan debuted an all-new Chevrolet Camaro for his 1967 US tour. Again, his main sponsor was Blair's Speed Shop in Pasadena, California. Bovan found out that touring was a little harder in 1967, as there were more funny cars emerging from the Midwest and East Coast. Being from California helped Bovan secure bookings, because the promoters liked the East versus West factor. What better draw than to arrange match races at local drag strips that pitted the East Coast against the West Coast? This was true no matter where the track was.

Seeing dollar signs in the new world of funny car racing, the fuel altered team of Snodgrass and Mahnken made the switch. The duo replaced their Fiat body with a Ford Mustang shell and a 427 Ford SOHC (single overhead cam) engine and went funny car racing. Larry Barker was the chosen one behind the controls of the "Psycho" Ford Mustang. The high-gear-only Mustang scored its biggest win not at a funny car event but at the 1967 Hot Rod Magazine Championships in Riverside, California. There they took home top honors in the competition eliminator. Since there was no class for funny cars, the Mustang had to enter the competition eliminator class to race.

To say Jack Chrisman ran his Comet on kill every run would have been a vast understatement. Here, at Bakersfield, Chrisman had a major blower explosion that removed the roof of his Comet funny car; however, he got the now-topless Comet stopped safely. Chrisman was okay and had plenty of parts, bodies, and pieces from Fran Hernandez at Mercury to get the car back in action.

Jack Chrisman was a transplanted "Okie" who begin racing at 23 in 1953. During his extensive career, he drove fuel and gas-burning dragsters, and he even drove for speed king Mickey Thompson. In 1961, he was an NHRA world champion, in a dragster, of course. His biggest contribution to organized drag racing was the stock-bodied blown nitro-burning Sachs and Sons "Super Cyclone" Mercury Comet. It was the world's first nitro-burning funny car, which he introduced in 1964. He is the proud "father" of the funny car.

A young unknown junior fuel racer and automotive artist named Kenny Youngblood came up with this ad for *Drag News* in 1968. This Lions ad was a first for Youngblood, and it would be the start of a star-studded art career for him in the automotive world. He still sells his prints online.

Charlie Allen was considered funny car racing's "all-American boy." His boyish good looks won over many a female drag fan. Allen started racing in the super stock ranks but quickly jumped into funny cars in late 1966–early 1967. His most popular funny car was his 1968 Dodge Dart sponsored by Saddleback Dodge. Charlie's Dart was also the test car for Crower racing products out of the San Diego area. In 1972, Charlie set the NHRA funny car speed record at 222.27 miles per hour in his 1972 Dodge Charger funny car.

Everything was new for Gene Ciambella in 1968. An all-new Pontiac Firebird funny car replaced the now NHRA-banned Destroyer Jeep. Also new for Ciambella in 1968 was that he changed his last name to Conway. The reason for this was that he tired of racers and announcers calling him "Cinderella." Therefore, Gene Conway, the funny car racer, was "born" in 1968.

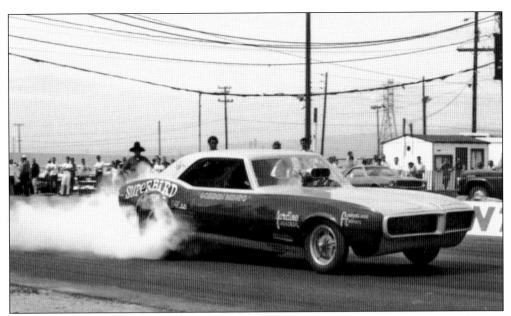

Gordon Mineo hit the SoCal funny car scene in 1968 with his "Superbird" Pontiac Firebird funny car. Gordon, with wife Ann and father Joe Mineo, toured SoCal and NorCal drag strips with their family-run Pontiac funny car. The Superbird became a fan favorite in Southern California and soon hit the national touring road for funny cars.

Wendell Shipman left the family carpet business and went funny car racing in 1968. Shipman's 'Cuda was powered by a 392 Chrysler Hemi built by "Flamin'" Frank Pedregon. When it got too costly to race his own car, Wendell could be found driving other funny cars. He drove for the Plueger Bros. and Griffis, Nathan Valdez, and Big John Mazmanian over a three-year period.

Norm Cowdery made the leap from his blown Austin Healy AA/MSP to a Camaro-bodied funny car in 1968. Cowdery's "Blue Fox" started running well at SoCal funny car events, but fate stepped in, and the Blue Fox burned to the ground—not once but twice. This ended Cowdery's brief funny car career, but there was always golf, Cowdery's other go-to sport.

Don Nicholson was now racing a new "Eliminator II" Comet for 1968. Gone was the 427 Ford SOHC injected engine, and in its place was a blown SOHC engine. This was an uneasy transition for Nicholson. He did not like superchargers, and two seasons later, Nicholson left the funny car ranks for the new pro stock class in drag racing. No blowers there— just carbs to tune.

AMC's big push into drag racing was in 1967–1969. "Banzai" Bill Hayes was at the wheel of the AMC-backed Grant SST "Rebel" funny car. But Hayes was not getting the results that the AMC factory people wanted in funny car racing. Hayes would be replaced by longtime drag racer Hayden Proffitt. Proffitt, a crafty old racer, had seat time in everything from fuel dragsters to super stocks, A/FXers, and funny cars. Proffitt did not set the world on fire with the Rebel, but he did give fans a show. At the 1968 NHRA US Nationals, during S/XS class run-offs, Proffitt did three huge wheel stands in one exciting run that put the crowd on its feet. Hayden did manage to run an 8.11 at 181.85 miles per hour that year for the car's best run ever.

Already in 1968, the funny car class was into recycling race cars. Here at Lions drag strip, the former Canuck Nova of Dale Armstrong and Frank Pedregon is now the Lorenz and Wright Nova funny car. Johnny Wright is at the controls of the roofless Nova. Wright would go on to drive Jim Shue's "Hellfire" Corvette in 1969 and one of Mickey Thompson's Mustangs in 1970.

After a spectacular two-car crash at Irwindale, both Randy Walls and the Pisano Brothers were looking to replace their destroyed race cars. Walls was looking to replace his Super Nova so he could finish out 1968's race commitments. Upon hearing this, Hayden Proffitt offered to sell his parked Corvair funny car. Proffitt was now racing for AMC and no longer racing the Corvair. Walls purchased the Corvair and was able to finish his commitments before debuting an all-new Bill Thomas–built Super Nova.

Garden Grove's Ray Alley no longer had his "Big Al" exhibition funny car; now he was at the wheel of his new Engine Masters 'Cuda funny car. Alley's 'Cuda was a regular at funny car shows in SoCal and NorCal. His 'Cuda would be the first in a long line of Engine Masters funny cars. Alley took an unknown Texas top fuel driver named Kenny Bernstein and showed the young Texan how it is done in a funny car in 1970.

Unfortunately, in 1968, San Diego's Johnny Hoffman became SoCal's first funny car fatality. The 26-year-old was driving Sheldon Konblett's "Snoopy" Jag-bodied funny car at Lions when he lost control near the finish line. The ensuing crash proved fatal for Hoffman. Before driving Snoopy, Hoffman drove in the top gas dragster class.

Glen Solano's "Invader" 'Cuda made its debut in the late 1960s and was an instant hit with SoCal funny car fans. Piloted by "Mighty" Mike Van Sant, the 'Cuda was a regular at SoCal drag strips. What made the car special was its paint and lettering design. Good friend Kenny Youngblood did the design, and his special alien invader on the side of the car delighted young and old. The little alien became the car's trademark and could be seen on all future Invader funny cars.

When "Big" John Mazmanian left the gas coupe class, he did it in style with his Pat Foster–built candy-red 1968 'Cuda funny car. A 426 Plymouth Hemi for power was tuned by Doug "Cookie" Cook and driven by Dave Beebe. Mazmanian was ready for the SoCal funny car battles at local drag strips. Soon after the car's debut, Dave Beebe stepped aside for John's nephew Rich Siroonian to drive the candy 'Cuda. Siroonian drove the 'Cuda to a final-round victory over Chicagoland's Don Schumacher at OCIR's 1968 funny car manufacturers' race. Siroonian ran the best 7.30 at 192 miles per hour at that event. Mazmanian's '71 'Cuda was the first funny car to run 220 miles per hour.

Ronnie Runyan went for a new Chevrolet Corvair in 1968. Dick Fletcher built the Corvair, and it was powered by a big block Chevy engine on nitro, of course. Runyan relocated to the Kansas City area to be closer to match race action, and he also opened Ronnie's speed shop. His Corvair ran the best of 7.83 at 187 miles per hour before he replaced it with an all-new Vega funny car. When Runyan was busy at his speed shop, brother Mike Runyan could be found behind the wheel of the Vega match racing in the Midwest.

Recycle time again—this time, it is one of Jack Chrisman's Comets finding new life as Dee Keaton's "Keaton's Komet." Keaton ran a blown 427 Ford SOHC engine on nitro in his new/old Comet. He also was a regular at SoCal funny car events in 1968. Keaton raced his Comet for a short while and then became a partner in the Stone, Woods, and Cooke Ford Mustang funny car in 1969 and 1970.

At the 1968 NHRA Winternationals in Pomona, California, fearless Fred Goeske debuted his all-new front-engine Hemi 'Cuda funny car. The car was built by Ronnie Scrima and Pat Foster at Exhibition Engineering. Goeske made a few test runs at Pomona and then, the following week, won the first race that the car would compete in, which was at Lions in Wilmington, California.

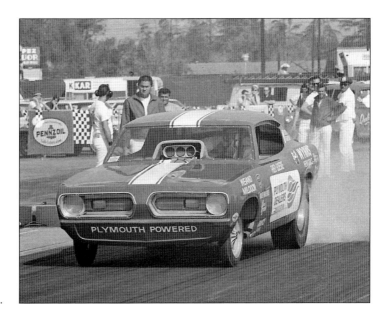

Riverside Raceway had "no burnouts" signs posted on its return road at the 1968 Hot Rod Magazine Championships. This unnamed, unpainted, new SoCal-based Camaro roadster's owner decided to ignore the signs and did burnouts on the return road. This is the result of ignoring the signage: one very bent Camaro roadster and a very hurt wallet. The car was not rebuilt, and the owner went top fuel racing after disposing of his bent funny car.

Doug Thorley's potent Chevrolet Corvair was all new, but Earl Wade and Dick Bourgeois toured the car for Thorley. Doug's business had taken off, and he was needed to help run the day-to-day operation. With Wade tuning and Bourgeois driving, the duo match raced the Corvair from the West Coast to the East Coast and in between in 1968.

Mickey Thompson's "Mach 1" funny car team made its debut at the 1969 Bakersfield March Meet in Famoso, California. Danny Ongais drove the blue Mach 1 and had a very interesting weekend. First, the car was making a practice run when, at the finish line, the engine sucked a rather large bird down into itself via the injectors. The engine had to be torn down and everything cleaned, which took a good part of the evening. The crew did its job very well, as Ongais went on to defeat Big John Mazmanian's candy-red 'Cuda in the final to win the first-ever funny car eliminator at the March meet.

It was time for a change, and Tom Sturm did just that in 1969. Sturm left the Chevrolet funny car fold with his all-new "Swapper" Challenger funny car. The new car featured a blown Hemi on nitro with Dale "the Canuck" Armstrong at the wheel. This was Sturm's first-ever race car that was not a Chevrolet. To make the swap to Mopar complete, his Corvair was sold to Northeast racer Jim McIntyre.

It was a bad day for funny car racing on June 15, 1969, at the NHRA Springnationals in Dallas, Texas. Pat Foster, driving the red Mickey Thompson Mach 1 team funny car, suffered a rear-end failure while racing Indiana's Gerry Schwartz. Foster lost control and ended up sliding in front of Schwartz, where the two cars collided.

The ensuing crash took the life of the 25-year-old Schwartz. Foster was not injured in the crash but was hospitalized with deep shock over the accident. The red Mach 1 was not rebuilt, and Thompson only raced one funny car for the rest of 1969.

El Cajon's Randy Walls went all out in late 1968 with an all-new Super Nova funny car. The Bill Thomas–built race car featured a blown big block Chevy for power, making Walls ready for serious SoCal funny car racing. The Nova could be found racing in SoCal, NorCal, and Arizona. Walls's new ride also appeared on magazine covers for nationwide exposure. Not to be outdone by magazines were Randy and his then-wife, Cheri. The blonde beauty helped back up the Nova after those long smoky burnouts, giving male spectators something to cheer about.

When Candies and Hughes (C&H) had a big sale at the end of 1968, one of their Louisiana-based 'Cudas came to Southern California. Tom McEwen purchased one of the C&H low-mileage 'Cudas and made it his first official funny car. Then, in 1969, McEwen raced in both top fuel and funny car classes in SoCal and at national events throughout the United States. At the end of 1969, McEwen sold the 'Cuda to Atlanta's Julius Hughes. Hughes raced the car out of his Atlanta-based speed shop.

The "Bad Bascomb's Ghost" Nova was a family affair for the Bradford clan. The Nova was owned by Bill Bradford Sr. and driven by Bill Bradford Jr. On the crew was brother Rich Bradford. Together, the Bradfords stayed close to home, racing at SoCal drag strips and having fun in 1969–1970. When funny car racing started to get too expensive, the Bradfords called it a racing career. Many funny car fans wondered where the name of the Nova came from. As Bill Sr. explained, it was the title of one of his favorite 1930s Wallace Beery movies, *Bad Bascomb's Ghost.*

After destroying their Corvair in a two-car crash with Randy Walls at Irwindale, the Pisano Bros. needed another race car. Joe Pisano made Doug Thorley an offer he could not refuse and purchased Thorley's 1967 Corvair. The old Doug's Headers Corvair now became the new Pisano Bros. Corvair. But alas, Frankie Pisano gave up driving for a fuel altered driver named Sush Matsubara. Matsubara jumped into the new car and, just like that, stuffed it into the OCIR guardrail head-on. Sush was not hurt, but Joe Pisano's wallet ached. They came back with a brand-new Camaro funny car for 1970.

Jim Shue's Hellfire Corvette funny car was one of the most beautiful race cars in Southern California during 1969–1970. Shue's Corvette was driven by Johnny Wright and tuned by Steve Montrelli. Money and sponsorship issues caused Shue to park his funny car for good in mid-1970. This left Wright without a ride, but Mickey Thompson hired Wright to drive one of his four funny cars in 1970. Steve Montrelli also joined the Thompson funny car effort in 1971.

A big fan favorite in SoCal funny car racing was Don Kirby's Beach City Chevrolet Corvette roadster funny car. In 1969, the car was piloted by "Daring" Gary Gabelich, and at Irwindale the same year, Gabelich burned the car to the ground. Undaunted, Kirby brought out another Corvette roadster for 1970. Gabelich started the year out in the car but left to drive the "Blue Flame" land speed record car. Top fuel owner/driver Ronnie Goodsell was now Kirby's driver, and he also burned the car to the ground. However, he did it on the freeway next to OCIR as the car caught fire at the OCIR finish line. Goodsell spun the car and went backward through the lower shutoff area on fire, through a bunch of trees, crashed through an eight-foot chain-link fence, continued up a hill and onto the slow lane of the freeway, and there, the car burned to the ground. Goodsell was not injured, but Kirby got a littering ticket from a California Highway Patrol officer.

"Big" John Bateman (left) and Gerry Glenn (right) had a pleasant chat with NHRA division director Bernie Partridge at Sacramento in 1969. Bateman soon left the top fuel dragster class and entered the wacky world of funny car racing. He raced funny cars from 1971 to 1973, starting with a short-lived 'Cuda, then a Ford Maverick, and finished his drag racing ownership career with a Ford Mustang. Glenn was driving in top fuel and funny cars at the same time in 1971–1973. He was the driver for the Plueger and Gyger Mustang as well as the Glenn and Glenn Charger funny car. But from 1970 to 1973, he also drove the Schultz and Glenn front-engine and rear-engine top fuel dragsters. In 1971, Schultz and Glenn won the NHRA world finals in top fuel at Amarillo, Texas. To say Glenn was busy at drag strips would be a vast understatement.

Southern California's "King of Speed" Mickey Thompson went funny car racing in a big way in 1969. His twin Ford Mach 1s were state of the art in the funny car class that year. Both cars were built by John Buttera and Pat Foster and featured dragster-style chassis and zoomie headers for better traction. Neither had ever been tried in the funny car class. The cars featured supercharged 427 Ford SOHC engines on nitro. Sadly, the red Mach 1 was destroyed in a two-car accident in Dallas, Texas, in June 1969. The blue Mach 1, driven by the "Flyin' Hawaiian" Danny Ongais (pictured), continued to dominate the funny car class wherever it raced throughout the United States in 1969.

SoCal's Donnie Hampton put his top gas dragster aside and went funny car racing in 1969—well, kind of. Hampton's "Too Bad" Corvette featured two blown Chevrolet engines side by side. His one-of-a-kind funny car ran on 100 percent alcohol and only as an exhibition funny car in Southern California. Hampton took his Too Bad to Australia in 1970, and there, his Corvette was destroyed in a two-car accident. Hampton was not injured in the crash and returned home sans his twin-engine funny car. The 'Vette was not rebuilt, and Donnie returned to racing his top gas dragster and building custom superchargers for SoCal racers.

NHRA may have banned Jeep-style funny cars in 1967, but Ed Lenarth did not care. The Long Beach–based Lenarth had raced the first Jeep-style funny car in 1966–1967 with the Lenarth and Wolford Secret Weapon. Now, late in 1968, he and Brian Chuchua got together and built the Holy Toledo Jeep-bodied funny car, also known as "the big yellow brick." The Toledo was built on a brand-new 120-inch Fletcher automotive chassis with a Lenarth-built 392 Chrysler Hemi. The yellow brick ran a dragster-style high-gear-only transmission, with Lenarth at the controls. For almost two years, the Holy Toledo raced every weekend at a drag strip in Southern California. The NHRA did ban Jeep funny cars at its national events but not at local events in SoCal.

Jack Chrisman drove his own Ford Mustang funny car in Southern California in 1970. Gone were the perks and factory sponsorship from Mercury. This ended up being Chrisman's final year of racing but not the last car he would build. In 1971, Jack built a sidewinder-style Ford Mustang funny car. The car was a rear-engine funny car that had its engine sideways and was chain driven. Chrisman never ran the car, and it was sold to Orange County resident Roy Mehus. With the car sold, Chrisman retired to his very successful business of building race car rear ends in his North Long Beach garage.

This was another case of "what's old becomes new again." Blower-builder Mert Littlefield took delivery of Northwest's Mike Miller's low-mileage Dodge Dart funny car in early 1969. Littlefield revamped the used funny car with a new engine and paint for his new "Rapid Transit" Dodge Dart funny car. Littlefield was a "homer" and pretty much raced in SoCal with his Dart. Late in 1970, he replaced the Dart body with an all-new Dodge Charger body. Unfortunately, the Charger burned to the ground in 1971, but Littlefield returned to funny car racing late in 1971.

# Two

# Innovation and Growing, the Funny Guys!

In the early days of Southern California funny car racing, funny cars were often pitted against fuel altereds. Things could get very exciting when the two classes were paired off. Here, the Mondello and Matsubara fuel altered Fiat is racing the New Breed Firebird funny car at Bakersfield in 1969. Sush Matsubara seems to have his hands full with the wayward Fiat, while Rusty Delling is straight and true with the Firebird.

Bob Pickett's funny car career started with his early-model Corvette. The blown 'Vette was a regular at Southern California drag strips in 1967 and 1968. Pickett went with a new AMX Javelin funny car for 1969. The move to an AMC funny car proved to be a bad one for Pickett. At OCIR, while making a run, the car took off at the finish line. As the car was flying, the body peeled off, sending the body-less car to the track surface. The impact of the car hitting the track broke Pickett's back, sending him to the hospital. Pickett returned in 1971 with an all-new 'Cuda funny car.

Clyde Morgan readied his EXP AMC Javelin funny car to hit the quarter mile. His Javelin was built by Fletcher automotive and featured a full suspension front and back. Morgan's Javelin was one of the first SoCal funny cars to break the 200-mile-per-hour barrier. Clyde's first funny car ride was in Charlie Wilson's Vicious Vette. He shared driving chores with a kid named Dale Pulde.

At the end of 1968, Doug Thorley became an AMC AMX factory-sponsored funny car racer. With his new sponsorship, he commissioned Fletcher Automotive to build him a rear-engine funny car for 1969. The new back-motor, Javelin-bodied funny car was driven by Bobby Hightower. That first summer, funny car driving was new to Hightower, and he flew the Javelin at the Irwindale finish line, standing it up on its parachute pack before going backward on its roof. The car spun on its roof and clipped the guardrail, causing the car to shed its body and flip upright on its wheels. It looked like Hightower was driving a very large go-kart straight and true down into the Irwindale shutdown area. Hightower was not hurt, but the car was beaten up, and the Javelin body was trashed. Thorley decided not to rebuild his flying Javelin. Hightower went back to driving top fuel dragsters that stayed on the ground.

Another AMC Javelin-bodied funny car for the 1969 season was "the Nutcracker," driven by Gary Read. Read was no stranger to nitro-burning drag cars. He drove top fuel dragsters and fuel altered roadsters before climbing into the cockpit of the Nutcracker. The Javelin was his first venture into the world of funny cars. Alas, the high-gear-only, Hemi-powered AMC product quickly faded into the funny car abyss of Southern California.

Drag racing's dance master was on a hot streak in 1969. Gas Ronda's Russ Davis Ford–sponsored Mustang ended 1969 with a victory in Sacramento's Governor's Cup race and then came home to SoCal and won the OCIR Manufacturers Race. Sadly, Ronda had the wrong kind of hot streak at the first race of the 1970 season. At Scottsdale, Arizona, he had a huge transmission fire at the finish line and severely burned his hands. The car was rebuilt, and Dick Poll drove while Ronda's hands were healing. However, he chose to retire after the 1970 season. The car was sold to fuel altered racer Dave Bowman.

Jess Tyree, also known as "Mr. Pontiac," was a master race car header builder, besides being a SoCal funny car owner/driver. In 1969, Tyree became the first American funny car owner/driver to race in Australia. His Pontiac-powered funny car rested on a Don Hardy chassis with the body painted by Molly. When Tyree was not racing in SoCal, he could be found touring his Firebird on the Coca-Cola Cavalcade of Stars throughout the United States in the summer months.

Larry Fullerton's first "Trojan Horse" funny car was in 1967, and he ran an injected nitro-burning Ford 427 SOHC engine. Fullerton got serious and added a blower to his Mustang in 1968–1969. Then, in 1970, his Mustang became a Ford Maverick sponsored by Galpin Ford. However, the Mustang body returned along with a new partner, Kevin Doheny, in 1971. With Doheny helping finance the Trojan Horse, the team began to both tour and win races locally.

53

Another funny car racer switched to an AMC Javelin body for 1969: it was Marv Eldridge's Fiberglass Trends funny car going AMC. Since Eldridge made funny car bodies, he got a great deal on a new body for his funny car. When Eldridge was busy with his booming business, his longtime friend Rusty Delling drove the Javelin funny car. Eldridge did drive the Javelin when he could get away from his business. In fact, he had the best time and speed in the car at 8.22 and 183.24 miles per hour—not too bad for an old-style 1957 392 Chrysler Hemi.

With the lure of large cash payouts in funny car racing in Southern California, the team of Walker and Geary made the switch to the new class. They removed the 1923 T body from their fuel altered and bolted on an AMC Javelin body, and it became an instant funny car. Tom "I Can Drive Anything" Ferraro was at the controls of the AMX-1 funny car. A short wheelbase, Chrysler Hemi power, and high gear only made the car outdated for 1969. Still, the AMX-1 did run at local SoCal funny car shows, mainly collecting first-round runner-up money.

In 1968, the team of Dick Bourgeois and Earl Wade raced the all-new Doug's Headers Corvair funny car nationwide for Thorley. With the switch to AMC in 1969, the Corvair body was replaced with an AMC Javelin body. Since Thorley's rear-engine AMC Javelin crashed mid-season, team Thorley was down to one funny car when the rear-engine car was not rebuilt. When AMC left drag racing, the Javelin body was replaced with a Chevrolet Vega body.

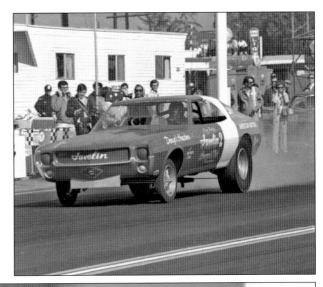

Roland Leong's first "Hawaiian" funny car was built on a Stage II chassis by Michigan's Logghe Bros. A full-size Dodge Charger body by Ron Pellegrini sat on the Logghe chassis. Keith Black supplied the 426 Chrysler Hemi. Leong debuted his Charger at the 1969 NHRA Winternationals in Pomona, California, with Larry Reyes at the helm. It was a spectacular debut, as the full-size Charger took off and flew at the Pomona finish line. It landed very hard on the track surface, staying upright, but the body and chassis were totaled. Reyes had a sore back and was incredibly lucky. A few weeks later, Leong returned with an almost-new mini Charger-bodied Hawaiian funny car. They won three races in a row on the first weekend of racing the car.

Before there was "Jungle Pam," there was Cheri Walls. The buxom blonde was the wife of the El Cajon–based funny car racer Randy Walls. Cheri delighted the male funny car fans when she got out on the track and helped back up Randy after one of his long smoky burnouts with the Walls family Nova funny car. Rumor had it that Cheri had offers from several men's magazines to pose au natural, but she turned them all down.

World War II veteran Charlie Wilson was one of the first SoCal racers to go funny car racing. Wilson's Vicious Vette, a blown 1958 Corvette, was a welcome sight at local SoCal drag strips in 1966–1967. In 1968, Wilson went with a Camaro-bodied funny car, the "Vicious Too." Wilson's funny cars gave rides to unknown drivers like Clyde Morgan and a kid named Dale Pulde. Both gained needed driving experience in those early days of SoCal funny car racing.

"Fearless" Fred Goeske traded his 1968 'Cuda body for a one-of-a-kind Plymouth Road Runner body in 1969. Having the only Road Runner funny car assured Goeske many more match race bookings across the USA. Fred did more than match race his Road Runner; he raced and won the first ever *Popular Hot Rodding* magazine event at Martin, Michigan, in 1969. Goeske waded through a large field of funny cars to win funny car eliminator. For Goeske, the year did not end well, as his Road Runner burned to the ground before the year's end.

Canadian transplant Vic Morse earned the nickname "Flipper" at the 1970 Bakersfield March Meet when he put the all-new "Mister T Corvette" funny car on its roof at the finish line. Morse was not hurt, but the new Corvette was now a very used funny car, yet it was repairable. However, the repaired Corvette did not finish 1970 in one piece. At Lions, on September 26, Rusty Delling drove the Corvette as it exploded a transmission just before the finish line. Delling lost control and plowed into the guardrail almost head-on. The ensuing crash destroyed the Corvette and put Delling in the hospital. The car was never rebuilt, and Delling never drove again.

La Mirada fireman Jim Dunn and partner Joe Reath made the leap from top fuel into the land of SoCal funny cars in November 1970. They commissioned Woody Gilmore to build a chassis for their new funny car. The team went with a 'Cuda body and a 392 Chrysler Hemi for power. Their car was basic and frugal for a funny car, with no fancy paint or a lot of chrome. The power to the rear wheels was supplied by a dragster-style direct-drive unit. The Dunn and Reath funny car with Jim Dunn driving won three out of four races they entered at the beginning of 1971. This proved that keeping things simple can be a good thing in funny car racing.

Making waves in the ocean of SoCal funny cars was the Mako Shark Corvette funny car from 1968 to 1970. The "Shark" was owned by Jim Wetton and Don Cullinan, with the driving chores sometimes left up to Roger Wolford. Ronnie Scrima built the chassis, and it had a 392 Chrysler Hemi for power. One rare thing about this funny car was that the owners Wetton and Cullinan took turns driving at one point while racing the Mako Shark. When Cullinan left the team, he was replaced by Gary Afdahl. He also took his turn driving the 'Vette. From 1968 to 1970, the car had four different drivers.

The decade of the 1970s brought out quite a few "here today, gone tomorrow" funny cars. One of those was a beautiful Ford Mustang that belonged to Nathan Valdez. Not a lot is known about Valdez or his funny car. When the car ran, it was driven by Wendell Shipman, but the car soon vanished from the SoCal funny car scene. It is believed the car was sold and Valdez turned his interest in cars to custom street rods.

One of the more impactful driver changes in 1970 was when Pat Foster replaced Larry Reyes in Roland Leong's Hawaiian funny car. Reyes left the Hawaiian to drive for Big John Mazmanian and his candy 'Cuda. Foster's ride in the Hawaiian was a short-term deal with him moving on at the end of the year. In that decade, Foster drove the Fiberglass Trends Corvette, Mickey Thompson's red Mach I, the Hawaiian Charger, the "Damn Yankee" 'Cuda, the Atlas Oil Tool Ford Maverick, Barry Setzer's Vega, John Lombardo's Vega, the "Soapy Sales" Mopar, the "Chicago Patrol" Ford Mustang, the "Shady Gleen" Mopar, the Super Shops Arrow, and the Keeling and Clayton "California Charger" Ford Mustang. He also drove in top fuel in the same time frame.

The Beebe brothers Dave and Tim joined forces with two Utah racers, Dallas Ferguson and Dean Hofheins, to race the "Dodge Fever" Challenger in 1970. The car was based in Garden Grove and mainly raced in SoCal. Tim tuned and built the engines, and brother Dave was at the controls of the Challenger funny car. The California/Utah team raced for one season and parted ways at the end of 1970. In 1971, Dave Beebe drove the "Mr. Ed" Charger, and Tim Beebe built an all-new "Fighting Irish" Camaro funny car with Ron O'Donnell driving.

May 1969 was a bad month for Steve Bovan, as his Blair's Speed Shop Camaro crashed and he was badly burned. He spent several months in the hospital recovering from his burns. As he pondered his options for coming back from his accident, a Phoenix, Arizona, widowed schoolteacher, Evelyn Dugger, was about to invest her late husband's money in a new oil company, D-A Custom Oils. An old friend of Bovan's put the two together for the 1970 season, and the widowed schoolteacher sponsored a new Camaro funny car with Bovan at the controls. Bovan's new ride had an M&S Welding 124-inch chassis, a 426 Hemi for power, and a George Cerny paint job. Bovan and D-A Custom Oils were ready to tour in 1970.

Late in 1970, Dave Braskett and Gary Burgin deserted the blown gas coupe class and went funny car racing with a new John Buttera–built chassis complete with independent front suspension. The Camaro was powered by a 354 Chrysler bored out to 427 cubic inches. The J&E fiberglass body was a rolling masterpiece of art done by Nat Quick. The car did not disappoint, with a first time out of 7.10 at 208 miles per hour—not too bad for a couple of old gas coupe guys.

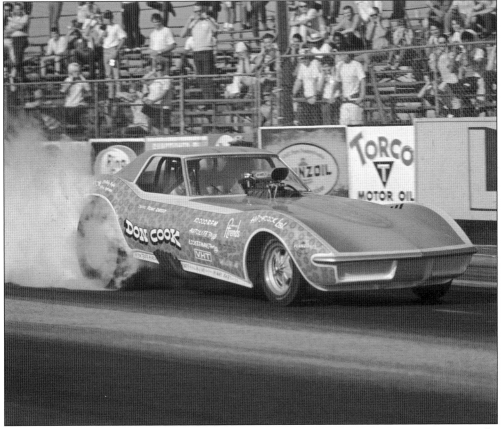

A cornerstone in SoCal funny car racing was Don Cook and his Corvette funny car. During the 1970 season, Cook and his Corvette seemed to be at every funny car event in SoCal. With Northwest transplant Frank Rupert driving, Cook's Corvette was always in the late money rounds and was a popular car with funny car fans. Rupert was no stranger to nitro-powered cars. He spent time behind the wheel of the "Eagle Electric," Pat Johnson's "Moonlighter," and the "Black Plague" top fuel dragsters before his funny car ride in Cook's Corvette.

Another veteran of SoCal top fuel racing was Kenny Safford. In 1970, he went funny car racing with the latest Stone, Woods, and Cooke Ford Mustang funny car. Besides Safford as the driver, a new Cooke replaced the old Cook. Abie Cooke was the new third partner in the SWC team. The former Cook—Doug Cook—became the crew chief on Big John Mazmanian's candy 'Cuda. Safford toured the SWC Mustang across the United States in 1970. The car was also a member of the Coca-Cola Cavalcade of Stars. At the end of 1970, Safford returned to his drag racing roots with a ride in Larry Bowers's all new top fuel dragster.

"Tricky" Dickie Olsen and Gordy Swearingen shared the driving chores of Olsen's Challenger funny car in 1970. The car raced out of Olsen's Competition Fiberglass business in SoCal. Olsen only raced his Challenger in Southern California because of his business. When his business started booming, he retired at the end of 1970 and called it a funny car career.

Warren Gunter's Durachrome VW Bug was a one-of-a-kind funny car in SoCal. The blown Chevy-powered VW Bug was a handful for Warren to drive, and the fans in the stands loved to watch the Bug make a half-mile run on a quarter-mile track. The short-wheelbase and high-horsepower Bug made each run an adventure for Warren and the fans in the grandstands. Warren did stuff his VW into a few guardrails in SoCal more than once, but then he would rebuild his mighty Bug after each incident. At one point, he lengthened his VW for better handling.

"Diamond" Jim Annin was a boat racer and a boat shop owner. When he got the urge to go funny car racing, he did it first class. Pat Foster was hired to build the chassis in late 1969. The chassis was built to the same specs as the 1969 Mickey Thompson Mach 1. A 426 Hemi by Keith Black was used for power. Keith Black's employee Mike Snively filled the driver's seat for all of 1970. At the end of 1970, the car was sold to Bob Papirnick, who renamed it the "Crosstown Challenger." Annin and Snively then went top fuel racing in 1971.

Barry "Machine Gun" Kelly was one of the few black funny car racers in the United States, and he was based in SoCal. Kelly and his Corvair funny car did not spend a whole lot of time racing in Southern California. As a black funny car racer, he was in demand at drag strips across the United States. Kelly could bring black drag race fans to fill grandstands, and promoters knew it was wise to book Kelly at their racetrack. The only time SoCal fans got to see Kelly was in the winter when he returned home from his long spring and summer tour.

Chicago and SoCal got together to race the Chapman Automotive Camaro in 1970. The Chapman Automotive funny car owners were looking for a crew to tour their funny car, which was being kept in Southern California without a crew to race it. Veteran top fuel racers Pat Johnson and Hank Clark answered the call; they were just what the Chapman people were looking for: experienced racers to drive their funny car. Johnson tuned the Camaro, and Clark did the driving. The third time they ran the car, it won the 1970 March Meet in Bakersfield, California. Not bad for a pair of funny car rookies.

It was a very bad day at OCIR in 1970 for the Hyder's garage Corvette funny car. Driver "Nitro" Nick Harmon walked away from this tangled mess after hitting the guardrail at speed. The Corvette suffered a transmission/clutch failure, which led to the accident. The car was brand new and had not even been painted or lettered. Glen Hyder returned to funny car racing almost two years later with a Camaro funny car. Harmon fielded his own funny car, the "California Rift Raft" Mustang, in 1971.

John Lombardo started his drag racing career with a 1955 Chevrolet stocker. Like many of his fellow drag racers, that type of race car was not fast enough. Lombardo solved his speed problem with a series of better, faster race cars. In 1969, Lombardo was racing a blown Corvette roadster in the gas coupe class in SoCal, then the funny car bug bit him. In 1970, Lombardo was in a wildly painted Dodge Challenger funny car. Of course, Lombardo had a nitro-burning Hemi under the body of his Challenger. Lombardo became a regular at SoCal funny car events in 1970, and his multicolored funny car was a hit with the fans. He mainly raced in SoCal because of his auto parts business. Good and bad things awaited him in his future funny car racing.

Unfortunately, 19-year-old Marc Susman used all his available funds to complete his state-of-the-art Chevrolet Nova funny car in 1969. Susman only ran his car a few times and then parked it for lack of funds. A phone call from "Jungle" Jim Liberman changed Susman's funny car future in 1969. Liberman was looking to purchase a third Nova to put on the match race circuit, as his team victory at the 1969 NHRA Winternationals had made him in demand on the circuit. In 1969, Susman became part of team Jungle Jim, and he stayed on to drive the Nova for Liberman. Then, in mid-1969, Susman crashed and totaled the Nova while match racing. Marc was not hurt, but the Nova was trashed. Liberman did not rebuild the Nova, and Susman returned to Los Angeles.

Bob Pickett started his funny car career in a blown early-model Corvette. He then joined the unofficial flying funny car club. With his airborne AMC Javelin-bodied funny car, he took flight at OCIR in 1969. While in flight, the body peeled off, and Pickett and the body-less funny car came crashing down to earth very hard. The impact broke his back, but he did keep the body-less car upright. Pickett returned to funny car racing after his back healed with a new 'Cuda funny car. He raced his 'Cuda for about a season and a half before accepting the driver's position in Pete Everett's "Lil Demon" funny car. With that, Pickett sold his 'Cuda to the Evans Bros. in Ohio and drove for Everett the next three seasons.

Arnie Behling crashed Mickey Thompson's Ford Maverick funny car while racing Pat Minick driving the "Chi-Town Hustler" on April 30, 1970, at Atco, New Jersey. Behling blew a front tire, and it sent the Maverick into the woods that adjoined the track. There, in the woods, the car flipped and destroyed itself, and Behling emerged without a scratch. He returned to SoCal sans one Maverick funny car. Then on June 21, 1970, at Lions drag strip, Behling drove Mickey Thompson's Mach 1 Mustang into the guardrail head-on and flipped the car. The car proceeded to slide upside down on fire down the racetrack. Once again, Behling emerged without a scratch, but the Mach 1 was trashed. It was only the first half of 1970, but Thompson had already lost two of his four funny car teams.

The Plueger Bros. and Griffis Corvette was one of those "here today, gone tomorrow" funny cars. The SoCal team debuted in 1970 with Wendell Shipman at the controls. The Steve Plueger–built Corvette quickly fell victim to the so-called Corvette curse in the funny car class. The black beauty was destroyed in a one-car crash and not rebuilt. Two years later, the Plueger Bros. returned to SoCal funny car racing with the new Ford Mustang funny car.

At the OCIR Manufacturers Race in November 1970, Ray Alley tested the guardrails, and it resulted in one very bent Engine Masters Duster funny car for Alley. Nobody was hurt, but Alley's wallet and pride took a beating. He started the year with two funny cars: a Cougar and a Duster. The Cougar burned to the ground early in 1970 while also burning rookie funny car driver Kenny Bernstein's hands. With this accident, Alley lost his Duster to a crash at OCIR. To say 1970 was not a banner year for him would be a vast understatement. Alley returned in 1971 with an all-new John Buttera–built Ford Mustang.

Glen Solano and Walt Williams combined forces in late 1969 to produce the Invader Corvette funny car. The new car had a Mike Kase chassis and a Fiberglass Trends body. At first, the car was powered by a blown Chevy engine, but the Chevy soon gave way to a blown Hemi engine. Bill Nash was slated to drive, but at the last minute, Mike Van Sant replaced him. When the car left for the Midwest match race circuit, Gary Scow replaced Van Sant. While racing at Rockford, Illinois, the Invader Corvette burned to the ground. Scow was not injured, but the Corvette curse had struck once again.

Coming into the 1970s, the Halloran and Peppmuller funny car was something rare in SoCal: it was an all-Chevrolet funny car. The "Ivory Hunter" Camaro featured a blown Chevy engine. The Chevy funny car fans rejoiced every time the car ran, but rejoicing fans do not win races. Halloran ended up leaving the team and built a Hemi-powered Vega funny car for 1971.

Gene Beaver was a hardcore top fuel dragster racer for over 20 years. Some of his drivers were the who's who of SoCal top fuel drivers, like Jack Chrisman, Mike Snively, Bill Alexander, Jim Ward, Steve Carbone, Danny Ongais, Hank Clark, Nando Haase, Roger Wolford, Pat Foster, and Jungle Larry Faust. With his purchase of Nelson Carter's "Super Chief" Charger funny car, Beaver and the Condit Bros. entered the world of funny car racing. A little paint and lettering and the "LA Hooker" Dodge Charger was ready for SoCal funny car events in 1970. Beaver and Steve Condit tuned the car, and Bill Condit was the crew. In the driver's seat was ex–top fuel dragster pilot Dave Condit.

At one time, the supercharged gas coupe class was thriving in Southern California. With the popularity of funny cars, that all changed. Gas coupe racers like Stone, Woods, and Cook, Big John Mazmanian, Gene Conway, John Lombardo, Dave Braskett, Gary Burgin, and Junior Thompson made the big switch to the more lucrative funny car class. Ray Zeller had left the gas coupe class in 1970 with his brand-new "Midnight Skulker" 'Cuda funny car. Zeller's 'Cuda had a Keith Black 426 Hemi engine and an Race Car Engineering (RCE) chassis. The Black engine was a natural choice for Zeller, since he worked at Keith Black's shop in South Gate, and his choice for a driver was former top fuel driver Stan Shiroma. Before funny cars, Shiroma had seat time in the Hawaiian and Mr. Ed top fuel dragsters.

Playing crash test dummy at the 1970 NHRA Supernationals in Ontario, California, was Sush Matsubara. He was driving the Pisano and Matsubara Camaro funny car when he lost control and slammed into the concrete guard wall. The ensuing crash destroyed the Camaro, but Matsubara walked away without a scratch. NHRA photographer Leslie Lovett was not as lucky; he suffered a broken ankle from flying debris pitched at him by the wayward funny car. Pisano and Matsubara did return in 1971 with a new Vega funny car.

All new for 1970 was Mickey Thompson's Ford Mustang Mach 1 funny car. The big changes in 1970 saw a 429 Ford Shotgun engine where the 427 Ford SOHC was in 1969. In the driver's seat was Mike Van Sant, as Danny Ongais left to go top fuel dragster racing. Ongais hooked up with car show guru Carl Casper to race Casper's "Young American" top fuel dragster for 1970. Engine problems plagued the new Mach 1, but those problems ended on June 21, 1970, when Arnie Behling, driving the Mach 1, stuffed the car into the Lions drag strip guardrail, destroying the car. Behling walked away from the accident uninjured, but the car was not rebuilt.

One of the few highlights in 1970 for Mickey Thompson was his white Ford Mustang funny car. Thompson had already lost his Ford Maverick and Mach 1 funny cars to violent crashes in the first six months of 1970. With Johnny Wright at the controls of the white Ford Mustang funny car, that car survived the full 1970 season of touring the United States.

There were huge changes in the world of drag racing and the funny car class in 1970. Tom McEwen convinced the marketing people at Mattel that funny car/drag racing would fit in with promoting their Hot Wheels diecast toy program. As the first major corporate sponsor, Mattel entered the world of funny car racing with the sponsorship of Tom McEwen and Don Prudhomme. Mattel's Hot Wheels Wildlife race team debuted at Scottsdale, Arizona, in January 1970 at the American Hot Rod Association (AHRA) Winternationals. Tom "the Mongoose" McEwen and Don "the Snake" Prudhomme each raced a funny car and a top fuel dragster under the Mattel Hot Wheels sponsorship.

With their Mattel Hot Wheels sponsorship in 1970, Don Prudhomme and Tom McEwen's Wildlife race team was a first-class operation. This was Prudhomme's first venture into the world of funny car racing. Prudhomme built his drag racing stardom in the top fuel dragster class from 1963 to 1970, but could he be a star in funny car racing? The funny car class was about to find out very quickly in 1970.

All new for 1970 was Ray Alley's Engine Masters Mercury Cougar funny car. This car had a one-of-a-kind chassis with the driver offset to the right of the engine, not like a standard funny car chassis in which the driver sits behind the engine. Alley had his good friend Kenny Bernstein drive the unique Cougar but not for long. The Cougar burned to the ground, and Bernstein suffered burns to his hands in the blaze. Alley decided not to rebuild the Cougar, and Bernstein healed to drive again.

Junior Brogdon brought out a new Phony Pony Ford Mustang funny car in 1970. Gone was Brogdon's junior dragster with a "Skinny" Ford Mustang body bolted on it with a blown 289 Ford engine. This was a standard-size Mustang funny car with a blown 392 Hemi. Brogdon raced his Mustang for a couple of seasons in SoCal and NorCal before retiring from funny car racing. He did return briefly in 1973 with a Ford Pinto pro stock named "Pee Wee."

"Lil" John Lombardo debuted his brand-new "Spider Web" Chevrolet Camaro at the NHRA Winternationals in Pomona, California, in January 1971. Lombardo always seemed to be the funny car owner/driver with the most outrageous paint scheme. This Camaro was one of a kind. However, it did not last long. Three months into 1971, the car became a fiberglass inferno at OCIR. Lombardo barely made it out of the melting/burning Camaro. His burns put him in the hospital for months, but Lombardo vowed to return. As he was recovering, his pal and chassis builder Steve Plueger visited him in his hospital room. There the two planned out Lombardo's new Vega for 1972.

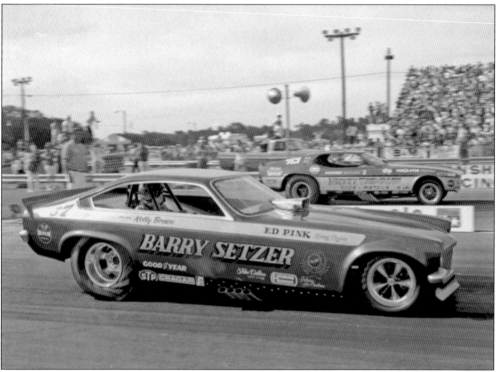

In 1971, Southern California and North Carolina joined forces to compete in the world of funny car racing. Double-knit tycoon Barry Setzer took delivery from John Buttera of a complete turnkey Chevrolet Vega–bodied funny car. Southern California also supplied the driver, Kelly "the Controller" Brown, to drive the candy-red Vega. However, Brown was only a temporary solution for a driver. His stuntman and business commitments prevented him from touring. This opened the driver's seat to Pat Foster, who became the car's official full-time driver. Although the car was owned by North Carolina's Setzer, it was based in SoCal during the winter months. A little-known fact is that after Brown left the driver's seat, Don Schumacher drove the Vega at a few SoCal funny car events in 1971.

Not many funny car fans got to see the Beaver and Condit LA Hooker Ford Maverick–bodied funny car run. The Maverick made its debut at the 1971 AHRA Winternationals in Scottsdale, Arizona. Three months later, for some unknown reason, the body was sold to Midwest funny car racer Danny Miller. Miller ran the body on his "Plastic Fantastic" funny car until he blew the body off. Meanwhile, the LA Hooker guys switched to a Ford Mustang body. So the LA Hooker sported Dodge Charger, Ford Maverick, and Ford Mustang bodies over a two-year period.

Coming out of the Chicagoland area was Ron "Snag" O'Donnell. O'Donnell had proven he could handle a nitro-burning race car when he drove the Denison, Arlansky, and Knox fuel altered to many wins in the Midwest in the mid-1960s. He then jumped from a fuel altered to the Chapman Automotive Camaro funny car in 1967–1968. O'Donnell headed to SoCal and ended up behind the wheel of Don Cook's Damn Yankee 'Cuda and then Tim Beebe's Fighting Irish Camaro. Ron's other claim to fame was when he was 12 years old, he became the national yo-yo champion for the United States.

A couple of fuel altered guys, John Hovan and Tom Ferraro, went funny car racing. Hovan at one time was a partner in the Way, Hovan, and Okazaki (soon to be) "Groundshaker Jr." fuel altered. Tom Ferraro drove just about every fuel altered in SoCal and, in his spare time, drove in top fuel also. Together, in 1971, the duo raced the deep purple Ford Mustang funny car in SoCal and NorCal. When Ferraro left the team, Grant Meredith left the gas coupe class and drove Hovan's Mustang in 1972.

Businessman Ed Wills was a top fuel hydro boat and top fuel dragster owner/racer, and his business was making fiberglass boats, trailers, and funny car bodies at his headquarters in Fresno, California. When Wills decided to go funny car racing in 1971, he wanted the best driver available, and that was SoCal's Dave Beebe. Beebe had just finished a stint in the Dodge Fever Challenger and was looking for a local funny car ride. Due to his day job and family, Beebe did not tour, as he believed in making his family his priority. Wills hired Beebe to drive his Mr. Ed Dodge Charger funny car. In 1971, Beebe did share driving duties with Mike Snively and Kelly Brown when he had a family event to attend on a weekend.

Gas Ronda had been a centerpiece for Southern California's funny car scene since his first long-nose injected fuel-burning Mustang funny car in 1966. After having his hands burned badly at the start of 1970, he had a life-changing decision to make. For the rest of 1970, Dick Poll drove Ronda's Mustang at local and national events. At the end of 1970, Ronda made the call to quit racing because of his still-healing hands. Fuel altered racer Dave Bowman purchased Ronda's Mustang (sans the engine) in 1971 and went funny car racing with his new "California Stud" Ford Mustang funny car. Ronda opened a bar just down the road from Irwindale raceway. Its name was Gas Ronda's Funny Car Bar, and inside the bar was decorated with large pictures of SoCal funny cars in action shot by photographer Steve Reyes.

As brother Dave went off to drive for Ed Wills in 1971, Tim Beebe introduced an all-new Fighting Irish Chevrolet Camaro funny car for 1971. His Camaro featured a Fletcher chassis with a 398-inch tunnel port Mopar Hemi and, to get the power to the back slicks, a B&J two-speed transmission. Chicago native and Irishman (of course) Snag O'Donnell was in the driver's seat of the beautiful green-and-blue-striped Camaro for most of 1971.

This is a father and son enjoying a day at the drag races, but not just any father and son. Top fuel and funny car driver Frank Rupert and his son Jason are watching the action at Irwindale raceway. In 1970, Frank had driven Don Cook's Corvette funny car the entire season. However, in 1971, Frank made the switch to being part owner of the Bays and Rupert Black Plague funny car. His new ride was a Chevrolet Vega–bodied funny car, and it was the first funny car in Southern California to use a Vega body.

There were big changes for Don Cook in 1971. Gone was his Corvette funny car, and in its place was a new 'Cuda-bodied funny car, the Damn Yankee. The new car featured an RCE Woody Gilmore chassis, an Ed Pink 426 late-model Hemi engine, and a Mr. Ed 'Cuda body. Don Kirby did the paint, and Kenny Youngblood lettered the red, white, and blue body. Driving for Cook was Pat Foster and Snag O'Donnell in 1971.

"Flash" Gordon Mineo was 25 years old in 1971, and out of those years, he had been racing for 10 of them. In that time, he had owned and driven a junior fuel dragster, two altereds, and five funny cars. Then in 1971, he had his strangest race car ever. After blowing off three Pontiac Firebird bodies in three weeks, he was out of bodies for his funny car. Always the racer, Mineo slapped a few sheets of aluminum and a wing over the roll cage on his now body-less funny car. Gordon's instant top fuel dragster was ready for the top fuel dragster class. Mineo entered his makeshift fueler in a Lions 16-car top fuel show, qualified 14th, and won his first round. The next week, the car returned to being a funny car with a new Pontiac Firebird body.

Gene Conway already had his Destroyer Jeep funny car banned by NHRA at the end of 1967. When he returned in 1968 with a Pontiac Firebird funny car, he raced for two seasons. Late in 1969, Conway introduced a new Corvette roadster-style funny car to SoCal funny car racing. So, of course, NHRA banned the roadster-style funny car from NHRA events. Conway thumbed his nose at NHRA and raced his roadster the entire 1970 and 1971 seasons. Then, in 1972, Gene brought out a hard-top Corvette body so he could race at NHRA national events and Division 7 World Championship Series races.

With the success of Mattel's Wildlife drag race team in 1970, the best was yet to come for Don Prudhomme and Tom McEwen. After selling his 1970 Hot Wheels 'Cuda to New Jersey's Sam Miller, Prudhomme unveiled a new 'Cuda in 1971. His new Hot Wheels 'Cuda featured a John Buttera chassis, Keith Black half-inch Stroker 426 Hemi, and Mr. Ed fiberglass body. Its third time out, the "Snake" 'Cuda recorded a 6.70 elapsed time for the 1,900-pound funny car. It was going to be a long year for other drivers and owners in the funny car class, as the Snake was ready to strike.

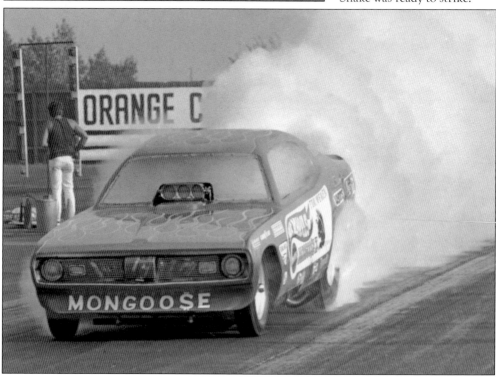

The "Mongoose" was on the loose in 1971. The other half of Mattel's Wildlife racing team, Tom McEwen, got his blank check from Mattel and went on a spending spree. A new John Buttera chassis and a Ramchargers 426 Hemi were his first purchases for Tom's new Duster. A J&E fiberglass body came next on the list. Some paint and lettering, and the Mongoose was ready for 1971. Now, the Mattel Wildlife team of Don Prudhomme and Tom McEwen were on the prowl in the jungle of funny cars.

Just before retiring from racing at the end of 1970, Jack Chrisman built an all-new Ford Mustang funny car for 1971. This car was a unique sidewinder rear-engine, chain-driven Ford Mustang funny car. Chrisman never ran the car and sold it to Orange County resident Roy Mehus. Mehus hired fuel altered driver Bill Finicle to drive the Mustang during the shakedown run process at OCIR. On a Wednesday afternoon, Mehus and Finicle were to make three checkout runs, but on the second pass, Finicle stuffed the Mustang head-on into the OCIR guardrail. Bill emerged unhurt from the somewhat bent funny car. Mehus fixed his bent car and drove the car a few times before selling it. He sold it to two brothers, John and Louie Force out of Bell Gardens. They repainted the car and named it the "Nightstalker."

Another big company that went all into the funny car class was ITT Continental Bakeries, also known as Wonder Bread. Promoted by Don Rackmann's Action Company in Westminster, California, the two-car team featured Chevrolet Vega panel bodies painted like a loaf of Wonder Bread. The "Wonder Wagons" also featured John Buttera chassis, 426 Hemi power, and Kirby and Youngblood paint and lettering. To fill the driver's seats were Kelly Brown and ex-altered pilot Glen Way. Not all went well during testing for the duo panels with one car being totaled at OCIR. This would leave Glen Way without a ride and only one Wonder Wagon, with Kelly Brown, racing in 1972.

Bellflower, California, was the home base of the "funny car factory" in 1971. The factory was a joint effort by Don Kirby, John Buttera, Nat Quick, and Kenny Youngblood to provide a one-stop shopping place for funny car racers. Kirby and Buttera supplied fiberglass bodies, paint, and chassis. Kenny Youngblood and Nat Quick were the in-house artists who designed and applied lettering with Kirby's custom paint. The business location was between Keith Black's shop in South Gate and Sid Waterman's engine place in Long Beach. All painting/lettering and fiberglass work was done at this location, while the funny car chassis building was done at John Buttera's shop about 25 miles away.

Chula Vista's Bill Leavitt was the "old guy" funny car racer in SoCal. As of 1972, he was the oldest owner/driver in funny car racing. The former top fuel dragster owner/driver was now at the wheel of his "Quickie Too" Ford Mustang funny car in late 1971. His Mustang was based on a 118-inch Byron racing chassis with a 1958 old-school 392 Chrysler Hemi engine. At Lions drag strip in December 1971, Leavitt recorded the quickest run ever for a funny car, 6.48 at 213 miles per hour.

SoCal's Joe Winter was unique to the funny car class in 1971. Another former top fuel dragster racer, he was the only one-legged driver in the class. Losing a leg to cancer did not stop Winter from driving his "Swinger" funny car. Here, at Fremont, a broken body latch at the finish line sent the body into the NorCal skies. It is an unofficial altitude record for a funny car body launch. Winter was not injured, but his Duster body destroyed itself upon landing. Winter returned quickly with a Mustang body for his Swinger funny car.

Roland Leong debuted his new Hawaiian Dodge Charger funny car in grand style at the 1971 NHRA Winternationals in Pomona, California. Leong's Hawaiian again took top honors in the funny car eliminator, making it two years in a row. New driver Butch Maas waded through a stellar field of competitors to claim top honors. Leong's new Charger featured a streamlined Logghe Bros. chassis with a Fiberglass LTD body. Al Bergler applied his metal-forming talent to making all the tinwork in the car. Of course, a Keith Black 426 Hemi was in the engine compartment, and Kirby and Youngblood took care of the paint and lettering of the blue-and-white Charger.

Making a big splash in 1971 SoCal funny car racing was the team of Bays and Rupert. Their Black Plague funny car was the first to utilize a Chevrolet Vega body in the funny car class. With Frank Rupert at the controls, the black Vega was a familiar sight at all SoCal funny car events. In 1973, the team switched to a 'Cuda body that had been purchased from Chicagoland's Don Schumacher. After the 1973 racing season concluded, the car was sold to former top fuel dragster racer Canadian Ken McLean.

In 1968, once again Mickey Thompson had an eye for talent when he hired an unknown Midwest junior fuel dragster pilot/chassis builder named John Buttera. Buttera teamed with Pat Foster to build Thompson's Mach 1 Ford Mustang funny cars for 1969. Buttera's revolutionary chassis design changed the future of funny car racing. Then, in 1971, Buttera opened his own chassis and fabrication shop, known as Lil John's Place. Buttera's race cars became the most sought-after in drag racing. His customer list read like the who's who in the world of funny car racing and top fuel. The talented chassis builder could also fabricate parts and pieces out of blocks of aluminum for customers.

John Bateman's Ford Maverick funny car did not have a very long lifespan in 1970. It first crashed while being towed down the return road at Irwindale. Then driver Pat Foster was trying to get the attention of a female spectator in the grandstands when the tow truck stopped but the race car did not. The car was repaired and left for its tour with new driver Marc Susman. In July 1970, Susman crashed and totaled the car in Rockford, Illinois. Susman was unhurt in the accident and returned to SoCal. Other drivers that drove the ill-fated Maverick in 1970 were John Collins and Gary Scow.

Mickey Thompson was at it again in 1971 with a Ford Pinto (pictured) and Ford Mustang funny cars. Both cars featured house-built chrome moly chassis and, for power, a 429 Ford Shotgun engine. Just as the cars were completed, Ford Motor Company canceled its contract with Thompson. This meant there was no more help from Ford to develop the engine for drag racing. Thompson realized he must switch to 426 Chrysler Hemis to stay competitive in the funny car class, and so both cars discarded the Ford engines in favor of the Chrysler product. Thompson also brought the first food-based product to drag racing with the sponsorship of Peter Paul candies. Twenty-year-old Dale Pulde (Pinto) and Henry Harrison (Mustang) drove for Thompson in 1971.

After switching to a complete Mopar funny car in 1970, Tom Sturm was back with a Chevrolet in 1971. His Camaro-bodied funny car was not all Chevy and had a 392 Chrysler Hemi under the Chevy body. It really did not matter much because the Hemi-powered Camaro crashed on this run at Lions drag strip in 1971. Sturm returned but not until 1973 with another Camaro funny car and then had very brief stint in SoCal.

# *Three*

# WE WILL ROCK YOU!

The Camaro funny car of the Adolph Brothers and Green was a one-of-a-kind funny car because of its chassis. Longtime dragster chassis builder Kent Fuller constructed this unique funny car-style chassis for the Adolph Brothers. Fuller, at the time, only built dragster chassis and components for dragsters. The body was a J&E creation that was painted by Bill Carter. The engine was supplied by fuel altered racer Don Green. Green took the Hemi right out of his fuel altered to race the funny car. With Jim Adolph driving, the team raced mainly in SoCal until the car was sold. It ended up in Hawaii and still races to this day as a bracket car.

Dave Braskett and Gary Burgin brought out their Buttera chassis KB Hemi Vega in late 1971. The Garden Grove, California, duo ran a great 6.73 elapsed at 218 miles per hour on their first weekend out. They won the first funny car event of 1972 at OCIR with their Vega. The following weekend, they flipped the car at Lions when their Vega crossed over and hit Joe Winter's Mustang in the rear quarter panel. The Vega rolled and flipped down the track, but driver Gary Burgin escaped injury. The Vega was repaired to race another day, and Joe Winter had minor body repairs to his Mustang. It was just another weekend of funny car racing in SoCal.

The San Pedro team of Bill Maggio, Lee Stuart, and Mike Thermos replaced their 1969 California Camaro funny car with an all-new Fletcher chassis, Paul Gommi 426 Hemi, and a Mr. Ed 'Cuda body in 1971. The "Sopwith Camel" 'Cuda funny car was ready to race in SoCal, with Mike Thermos at the controls. The team mainly raced in Southern California because of the members' "real" jobs and business commitments. The car did have one other driver for a short while: Ron Rivero of the "Frantic Four" top fuel team took a few laps in the Camel.

Sharing the 1971 AHRA Winternationals winner's circle in Scottsdale, Arizona, with Hurst's Linda Vaughn is Steve Montrelli (left) and Dale Pulde (right). The pair had just won the funny car eliminator with the new Mickey Thompson Pinto funny car. Pulde was no stranger to funny car racing, having driven for Charlie Wilson in the past. Besides funny cars, Pulde at eight years old was a national champion in quarter midget racing. He then drove a junior dragster at just 14 years old before venturing into the world of funny car racing. With Montrelli's tuning and Pulde's driving, Mickey Thompson's Ford Pinto funny car had great years in 1971–1972.

John Bateman was back again after he lost his 'Cuda and Maverick funny cars to crashes in 1971. Bateman, this time, returned with a new RCE-built Ford Mustang funny car. Chicagoland's Cliff Zink manned the controls of the multicolored Mustang. However, Zink was only temporary. John Collins assumed driving duties when Zink returned to the Midwest. Bateman and Collins raced for a few seasons until Bateman wanted to retire from drag racing. With that, John Collins purchased Bateman's entire funny car operation and became the sole owner/driver of the Mustang.

Funny car racers have that never-quit mind-set, or at least "Nitro" Nick Harmon did in 1971. After walking away from a horrific funny car crash in the Hyder's Garage Corvette funny car in 1970, he was back. This time, with his wife, Karen, he debuted a Ford Mustang funny car in 1971. Nick was not at the controls of the Mustang; Bryan Raines filled the driver's seat for the Harmons. Raines had parked his supercharged roadster gasser to go funny car racing with the Harmons. Raines had a short stint in the "California Rift Raft" Mustang. Nick Harmon resumed driving when Raines left to field his own Vega funny car.

At the end of 1971, the team of Dunn and Reath sold their 'Cuda funny car to SoCal resident Mike Diedrich. The pair went the innovative route with an all-new RCE/Woody Gilmore–built rear-engine 'Cuda funny car for 1972. The Dunn and Reath 'Cuda was not the first rear-engine funny car to race in the class, nor would it be the last team to try the engine in the rear. The biggest issue that the team had to solve or overcome was getting a rear-engine funny car to go straight for a quarter of a mile. That task fell in the lap of driver Jim Dunn. Could 1972 be the year of the rear-engine funny car?

The summer of 1972 was not kind to Burbank engineer Mike Halloran. He crashed and burned his Vega funny car at OCIR. Mike did walk away from the charred, tangled mess that once was a beautiful race car. Mike vowed to return, and at the end of 1972, he did just that. His new "Dodger Charger" funny car sported an RCE chassis and a Sid Waterman 426 Hemi. The first time out with his new racer, Mike clicked off a 6.73-second, 219.64 mile-per-hour run—no new car blues for Halloran.

This was a regular sight at winner's circles across America: the Barry Setzer Bunch; from left to right are Miss International Hot Rod Association (IHRA) Dianna Warren, double-knit tycoon and car owner Barry Setzer, Miss Longhorn Nationals, and driver Pat Foster. The combination of North Carolina's Setzer and SoCal's Pat Foster was a juggernaut in funny car racing in the early 1970s. Their candy-red Vega raced at NHRA, IHRA, and AHRA National events all over the United States. Add match racing to the mix, and that was one busy funny car team throughout the summer months. In the winter, the car was a fixture in SoCal and raced at open funny car shows all over Southern California.

From 1967 into the mid-1970s, SoCal drag strips were home to Pete Everett's line of funny cars. First up was his New Breed Firebird, then his Mercury Cougar–bodied New Breed funny car. In the early 1970s, he raced his Lil Demon funny car out of his Chevron service station in Southern California. Everett had Rusty Delling Jr., Leroy Hales, and Bob Pickett as drivers in that time period. The Lil Demon was a fan favorite whenever it raced in California or Arizona.

The interesting saga of Joe Pisano continued into 1972 with this semi-burn-down of his Vega funny car at Fremont, California. As of the end of 1971, Pisano had three funny cars crash, and one burned to the ground. Then, in 1972, the strange tradition of funny car destruction started up again. This incident was minor compared to previous failures; a body replacement, and his funny car was good to go. But alas, the new body was destroyed only a few weeks later at OCIR. His Vega sideswiped one of the OCIR guardrails and, once again, destroyed its new body.

Southern California surfer girl Susan Draper did a little modeling with Gary Hazen's "Panic" Vega funny car. This shoot was not an ordinary "pretty girl with a funny car" photography session. The folks at Roach Studios in Worthington, Ohio, took one of the images and used it on a t-shirt that was sold worldwide. Thus, Susan and Hazen's SoCal-based Vega were used to promote the sport of drag racing and funny cars all over the world.

The O'Neill brothers migrated from Canada and settled in Southern California. Soon after getting settled, the brothers went funny car racing with their "King Rat" Camaro. Gervase drove the all-Chevy-powered Camaro, while brother Johnny tuned their funny car. From 1972 to 1977, the O'Neill brothers could be found racing at SoCal drag strips. The King Rat was a big favorite with Chevrolet fans because of its all-Chevy stance; no Chrysler Hemi for these guys. The car ran the best of 6.72, which made it one of if not the quickest of all Chevrolet funny cars in the country.

From kid gofer to stud funny car driver is the story of Russell "Doughboy" Long. Russell was just a kid who loved drag racing and did odd jobs for racers when he attended the races. His hero was Tom McEwen, and he could be found at the races doing jobs for racers, but mainly for McEwen. Russell's real passion was to drive a funny car and, at 19 years old, that dream came true. With the help of McEwen, he obtained his NHRA funny car driver's license. For six years, Russell raced as a journeyman funny car driver. He drove for Tom McEwen, Jungle Jim Liberman, the Chi-Town Hustler, Don Schumacher's Wonder Wagon 'Cuda, Dennis Fowler's "Sundance" Monza, and Pat Brinegar's "Arkansas Razorback." His longest tenure was in Charlie Proite's "Pabst Blue Ribbon" Charger.

In March 1971, John Lombardo's Camaro burned to the ground at OCIR. John barely made it out of the burning fiberglass inferno alive. He did sustain serious burns that required a hospital stay. While in the hospital, chassis builder and good friend Steve Plueger visited Lombardo. There, in Lombardo's hospital room, Plueger and Lombardo drew up plans for John's next funny car, a Vega-bodied funny car. Lombardo debuted his new Vega in 1972. In fact, John and his Vega were featured in the movie *Drag Racer*, which was shot in 1972 at Irwindale and OCIR.

"Fearless" Fred Goeske went from a Mopar Duster–bodied funny car in 1971 to a high-flying Vega-bodied funny car in 1972. Another investment for 1972 was a set of wheelie bars for the new Vega. Here, at Irwindale, Goeske and his Vega give the fans in the stands a thrill with this high-flying wheel stand. A slightly bent chassis was the result of the Vega's flight and hard landing.

Mickey Thompson brought quite a few innovations to funny car racing. He introduced the dragster-style chassis and zoomie headers in 1969 with his team's Ford Mustang Mach 1s. Thompson also had failures in funny cars, like the monocoque chassis in 1970 and the titanium chassis–equipped Pinto in 1971. One of Thompson's biggest personal disappointments was not being able to get the 429 Ford Shotgun engine to work in drag racing. Then, in 1972, he introduced a Pontiac Grand Am–bodied funny car to drag racing. It was a distinctive-bodied funny car with the very talented Dale Pulde at the controls. The strangest thing about the car was not the body but its color. It started out yellow, then red, and finally black. Mickey could not seem to make up his mind about what color the car should be.

The very happy place to be at Irwindale, California, in 1972 was the winner's circle. The team of Littlefield and Sublett had just waded through a great field of SoCal funny cars to earn the right to be in the winner's circle at this event. From left to right are Mert "Sparky" Littlefield, Marty Sublett, Don Cook, and Irwindale manager Steve Evans. Their Vega was a regular at SoCal funny car shows in the early 1970s.

Longtime top fuel owner/driver Wayne "the Peregrine" King thought he would give funny car racing a chance in 1972. He debuted his brand-new unpainted Dodger Charger funny car at a two-day event at Irwindale. On a Saturday, King made two runs to shakedown the new car with no problems. Then on Sunday, the second run in the car was a disaster, as a fire at the finish line burned the chutes off. With smoke filling the car, King drifted off the side of the track and into the rather large boulders that lined the shutdown area. The rocks destroyed the chassis and burned body, totaling the car. Wayne was not hurt, but his new car, with only four runs on it, was junk. He returned to his top fuel roots and tried to forget about his venture into the funny car class.

Besides his Pontiac Grand Am funny car, Mickey Thompson raced a Vega-bodied funny car in 1972. The Vega was a special race car for Thompson, as it was the 78th race car that he had owned and raced. The Vega was built on an RCE chassis with a 482-inch late-model Hemi, and the body and paint were done by Don Kirby. Of course, it was sponsored by Peter Paul Candy, and driving chores went to ex-altered and top fuel driver Louisiana native Henry Harrison.

The team of Larry Fullerton and Kevin Doheny had a particularly good year in 1972. Not only did their Trojan Horse Ford Mustang funny car tour Australia, but they also won the NHRA World Championship in Amarillo, Texas. The Trojan Horse consisted of a John Buttera chassis, an Ed Pink late-model 488-inch Hemi, and a Don Kirby body and paint. As of 1972, Fullerton was credited with the quickest and fastest run by a funny car at an NHRA major event with 6.40 at 228.42 miles per hour.

Early in 1972, crew chief Dennis Larson and driver Mike Van Sant made checkout runs with the new Stone, Woods, and Cooke Ford Mustang funny car at Lions. The duo was getting the new car for a nationwide tour of match racing. Then, in September, at US 30 Dragway in Gary, Indiana, the Mustang was totaled in a spectacular accident. Driver Mike Van Sant was hospitalized with non-life-threatening injuries. Van Sant healed from his injuries, but could SWC recover from yet another destroyed funny car? The answer was yes, as the team returned in 1973 with a new Mustang funny car.

Hopping on the back-engine bandwagon in 1972 was Long Beach resident Robert Contorelli and his Ford Mustang funny car. The former top fuel racer spared no expense in building his Mustang. Contorelli put together an RCE chassis with a Donovan aluminum Hemi and an exclusive body made for him by Ed Wills, also known as "Mr. Ed." After the dust settled down, Contorelli had no funds to run his back-motor funny car. He did manage to run a few times with a best of 6.89, and then he parked the car. Contorelli ended up selling his Mustang to sand drag racers, and it became a sand-racing funny car.

SoCal funny car racers only choose the finest cuisine when on tour in California. The Keeling and Clayton team stopped at a NorCal Jack in the Box for a bite to eat in 1971. The crew at Jack in the Box wanted a better look at the Ford Pinto funny car, so the Keeling and Clayton team unloaded the car. The car was placed in front of the eatery for an impromptu car show, and Jack came out to mingle with driver Tom Ferraro, much to the delight of the restaurant patrons.

Upon hearing that NHRA had all but killed the fuel altered class, Bob "Blue Blazer" Hankins went funny car racing in 1971. At first, Hankins outfitted his "Blue Blazer" fuel altered with a mini-Corvette body for his first attempt at racing in the world of SoCal funny cars. Then, in 1972, Hankins tried again with a Ford Pinto–bodied funny car complete with a 392 Hemi. Hankins only raced for a brief time in 1972, as he retired at the end of the year. He sold his Pinto to the Ferguson brothers Dean and Vic. They, in turn, rebranded it the "Moonraker" Ford Pinto in late 1972.

Pleasing the crowd was always the goal for "Flash" Gordon Mineo. He delighted funny car fans by stuffing his 1972 Chevrolet Vega funny car into the OCIR guardrail head-on after a burnout. Mineo was not hurt, but his Mike Kase–built Vega was a bit shorter. After a quick trip to Kase's shop, the Vega was just like new and ready for its 1972 tour of the United States.

Gary Densham was officially the world's quickest and fastest high school auto shop teacher in drag racing. Densham achieved that title at the controls of the Densham and Walker Ford Pinto funny car. He was no stranger to drag racing or funny cars. The Densham and Walker Pinto was the second Pinto funny car he had driven. His first was the G&S Transmissions Pinto in 1970–1971. Densham came to the funny car class via the supercharged gasser class in 1969. There, he drove the Bilby, Densham, and Plueger blown Hemi roadster at gas coupe events in SoCal. And yes, he was a full-time high school auto shop teacher when he was not racing.

This version of the "Rat Trap" Satellite funny car was raced by Pomona residents Dennis Fowler, Gale Fowler, Don Green, and Charlie Handcock in 1972. The Pomona-based team had Dennis Watson build the chassis, and Sid Waterman supplied the Hemi engine. A new Mr. Ed Satellite body was painted by Bill Carter with Tom "I Drive Anything" Ferraro in the driver's seat. The team disbanded after only one season together.

"Nitro" Nick Harmon went back to driving his own funny car after Bryan Raines left the team to drive his own Vega funny car. Harmon tried to make a run in his California Rift Raft Ford Mustang funny car on three wheels at OCIR. Harmon had lost his left rear wheel while under full power, causing the car to veer into the guardrail. Harmon was not injured, but the car took a beating. The Mustang was repaired, but Harmon changed the name of his funny car to the "California Shaker"—maybe for good luck?

In the 1970s, there were not many female funny car owners. However, Myra Gelfand, also known as "Super Jewess," broke into the men's only owners club with her ownership of the Damn Yankee 'Cuda funny car. Gelfand took over ownership from Don Cook in mid-1972 and raced the car with Wayne Greiser as the driver. It turned out to be a short tenure for Gelfand, as the car was absent from SoCal in 1973.

The adventures of "Blazin'" Gary Hazen in drag racing could fill a storybook. Hazen raced his Panic funny car for two seasons (1972 and 1973) and ran the best of 6.13 at 231 miles per hour. In five total seasons of drag racing, besides his funny car, he ran a Panic fuel altered, a Panic top fuel dragster, and a Panic rear-engine top fuel dragster. The consensus was that Gary Hazen liked nitro racing.

Late in 1972, at Scottsdale, Arizona, Prudhomme and McEwen squared off as the Hot Wheels/Mattel Wildlife funny car team. This was the last time the two squared off as Wildlife team members. In 1973, Prudhomme took on Carefree cinnamon gum and Coca-Cola as major sponsors. McEwen's Duster had logos for Carefree peppermint gum and Coca-Cola splashed on its body. Mattel was still on both cars but only as an associate sponsor in 1973.

Jimmy Boyd's funny car career was very brief in December 1972. The low-dollar ex–top fuel racer built his "Red Turkey" 'Cuda funny car and tuned his own 392 Hemi engine. Boyd's first full run was also his last run in his 'Cuda. His Red Turkey funny car tried to self-destruct at the finish line at Lions drag strip. Boyd was not hurt in the explosion and mayhem, but the "Turkey" was totaled and not rebuilt.

The Glenn brothers and Bill Schultz went funny car racing in late 1972 with a Dodge Charger funny car. Gerry "the Hunter" Glenn was at the controls, and master engine builder and tuner Bill Schultz took good care of the nitro-burning Hemi that powered the Charger. In 1971, Schultz and Glenn were NHRA's world champions in top fuel, so their crossover to funny car would be no problem, right? The team did not gel in funny car racing and split in 1973. The next year saw the car re-emerge as the "Shady Glenn" Dodge Charger with Gary Burgin driving. Schultz and Glenn returned to their drag racing comfort zone of top fuel racing.

Glen Hyder's Camaro funny car was his follow-up to the ill-fated Corvette funny car that had been destroyed in a crash at OCIR in 1970. Hyder's "Outage" Camaro made its debut in 1972 at Irwindale with either Gary Southern or "Rocket" Rod Phelps driving. The car raced off and on in the 1973 season in SoCal. At the end of 1973, Glen decided that he could not afford the high cost of racing a funny car, and the car was parked.

*Car Craft* magazine's August 1972 issue featured funny cars from all over the United States. One of the cars pictured made big waves and not good waves. It seemed a Midwestern librarian was offended by the photograph and deemed it pornography. She pulled the magazine from the library and called the offices of *Car Craft* in Los Angeles. Of course, the *Car Craft* staff just blew her off as some crackpot and thought it was a joke. The staff was not laughing when she called and talked to the publisher. The staff was made to apologize for their transgression, but she still had the issue pulled from all the libraries in that Midwestern state. The photograph in question was Joan Trejo (driver Henry Harrison's girlfriend) posing with Mickey Thompson's Vega funny car.

Ed Wills introduced something new to SoCal funny car racing: a new mini Plymouth Satellite body. His Satellite body was a big hit with funny car owners nationwide, and of course, he had the first one on his Mr. Ed funny car. In 1972-1973, his Satellite saw plenty of action at Southern California drag strips and NHRA major events. During that time, the Mr. Ed funny car had a handful of drivers that included Dave Beebe, Kelly Brown, Mike Snively, and Bobby Rowe. At the end of 1973, the car was sold to Texas racer Mike Burkhart, and it raced in 1974 with Richard Tharp driving. Ed Wills went back to his first love: top fuel dragster racing in SoCal.

The "Time Machine" Vega funny car was owned by Bob Taylor from Costa Mesa, California. Prior to his Vega, Taylor had purchased Marv Eldridge's "LA Challenger" funny car and ran it as his first Time Machine. Johnny Wright and Denny Savage drove the "Challenger" until the Mike Kase–built Vega was ready to race. Savage drove the Vega first, but it was Harlan Thompson who took over driving duties when the Vega went on tour. At the end of its 1973 tour, the Vega was sold to Northern California racers.

The last drag race at Lions drag strip was on December 2, 1972, and it was also the last drag race for Big John Mazmanian. After the race, Mazmanian sold his complete funny car operation to Parnelli Jones and Vel Miletich. Driver Danny Ongais stayed on and drove the funny car and their new top fuel dragster in 1973. The Flyin' Hawaiian won the first two SoCal funny car events that took place in 1973 for the newly formed team of Jones, Miletich, and Ongais.

The racing outlook for Jim Nicoll and Chuck Tanko was looking pretty good for 1973. They had just bought the ex–Barry Setzer Vega to race for the season. Unfortunately, everything went sour at the NHRA Gatornationals in Gainesville, Florida. An engine failure followed by a huge fire that engulfed the Vega at the finish line destroyed the car. Nicoll struggled to escape the burning funny car. With the roof melting down on him, he crawled out the side window to safety. The car was a total loss, but Nicoll and Tanko returned to finish out the 1973 season.

Between January 1, 1973, and March 1973, eighteen funny cars either crashed or burned to the ground. Southern California–based cars on that dubious list were: Jim Nicoll's Vega, the Trojan Horse Mustang, Fearless Fred Goeske's Vega, Pete Everett's Lil Demon, the Rat Trap Satellite, and Mickey Thompson's Pontiac Grand Am (pictured). Thompson's Pontiac burned at the NHRA Gatornationals just before Nicoll's Vega. Driver Butch Maas suffered serious burns and lost a pinky finger in the inferno.

Jeff Courtie took "do it yourself" to the extreme with his 'Cuda funny car. Courtie built his own funny car from the ground up. He did everything from the chassis to the engine to the tin work and paint. This was not his first self-built funny car; his prior Mustang funny car was also a homebuilt production. Courtie raced in Southern California his entire racing career.

Paula Murphy's STP Duster funny car was built by Romeo Palamides. Romeo built the 118-inch chassis, and "Fat" Jack Bynum took care of the 426 Hemi engine. The body was a product of J&E fiberglass with paint by Dee Jay. As of 1972, Paula had 14 years of auto racing competition that included Bonneville, Mobil Oil economy runs, sports car rallies, and of course, drag racing. When Murphy sold her Duster, it went to England and was raced by Nobby Hills (owner) and Owen Haywood (driver) as the "Hound Dog" funny car.

After gaining experience from Gas Ronda's former Mustang funny car, Dave Bowman was ready to build his own funny car. Bowman chose the rear-engine design for his Vega panel funny car. He built his own chassis from a Woody Gilmore/RCE blueprint, and he also built the 1958 392 Chrysler Hemi engine. The Vega panel body was custom-made by J&E Fiberglass, and it took four months for Bowman to complete his California Stud funny car. A very serious highway accident curtailed Bowman's racing career in late 1973. His panel was sold and ended up as a sand funny car.

Joining Dunn and Reath, Robert Contorelli, and Dave Bowman in the rear-engine funny car revolution club was Burt Berniker and his "Hindsight" Duster. The Hindsight was the last rear-engine funny car to try and challenge the conventional-style funny car in Southern California. Jim Adolph and Dennis Geisler traded off driving the back-motored Duster in 1973 and 1974. The car went out in a blaze of glory at the 1975 NHRA Winternationals in Pomona, California. With Geisler driving, the Hindsight car did a backward flip off the starting line and destroyed itself. Geisler walked away from the tangled mess that once was a funny car, and Berniker did not rebuild.

Quite a few used funny cars got a new life in SoCal, and one of those was Dunn and Reath's first 'Cuda funny car. "Super" Mike Diedrich purchased the low-mileage 'Cuda and set out to do battle at local Southern California funny car events. Diedrich was just learning about driving his new purchase when he had a huge fire in his 'Cuda. He was so shaken up about the fire he decided it was not enjoyable and sold his 'Cuda.

The summer of 1972 made Jim Dunn a sort of movie star with a documentary filmed while he was on tour. *Funny Car Summer* chronicled a summer in the life of funny car racer Jim Dunn and the Dunn and Reath 'Cuda funny car. A film crew followed Dunn as he raced throughout the United States. The film was produced by John Brooks and Ron Phillips with Sandler film productions. It was filmed in 1972 and released in 1974 to rave reviews from the drag race community. The film brought forth the highs and lows of touring a funny car with no fluff, just the facts, about racing in 1972.

After brief partnerships with the Adolph Brothers in 1971 and Dennis Fowler in 1972, Don Green struck out on his own in 1973. The former fuel altered racer put his 426 Hemi in a Don Long chassis, slapped a Mustang body on it, and went racing. Longtime pal Jim Adolph drove the Mustang funny car. However, Green did not have the "green," or money, to race on a regular basis. A lack of money and sponsorship sidelined the Mustang in late 1973.

Another outcast from the fuel altered class was "Wild" Willie Borsch. Willie was one of the most popular fuel altered drivers in Southern California, with his one-arm driving style in the hardest race car to drive amazing drag fans. The folks at Revell model kits knew of Willie's popularity and made him an offer: if he supplied the engine, they would buy him a funny car. A deal was struck, and Borsch became a member of the gaggle of Revell-sponsored funny cars. So Borsch became Revell's "Wildman" in 1973 and went on tour with his Chevy-powered Dodge Charger funny car. The pairing of Willie and Revell received a lot of attention in the media, which Revell loved because it sold model kits. However, Borsch never did adapt to his funny car, and he soon faded by the end of 1973. He stayed in Michigan and drove for Walter Koch and his Walt's "Puffer" funny car.

Steve Plueger was no stranger to drag racing, as he was an expert chassis builder and funny car owner/racer. In 1969, he partnered with the Bilby, Densham, and Plueger gas class supercharged roadster that raced in SoCal. Then, in 1970, he built another car and partnered with the Plueger Brothers and Griffis Corvette funny car with driver Wendell Shipman. Late in 1972, Plueger was ready to go funny car racing again with a Ford Mustang funny car. Besides building the chassis, Plueger made sure the Mustang had all the best parts and pieces to withstand the year-round funny car events in Southern California. The Plueger Brothers and Gyger Ford Mustang supplied driving time for Dale Pulde, Gerry Glenn, and Dave Condit when it ran throughout 1973.

Jim Thomas's Genuine Suspension low-rider Ford Mustang funny car was an exceedingly rare sight in 1972. Thomas had the best parts that money could buy in his low-riding funny car, but the car rarely was seen at local Southern California events. When the car did run, Gary Read or Dean LaPole drove the Mustang. The car quickly disappeared into the SoCal funny car abyss, never to be seen again. In its place, Thomas debuted an all-new Genuine Suspension top fuel dragster in late 1973 with Gary "Mr. C" Cochran at the controls.

In the late 1960s, Joe Lee and Leonard Abbott raced in top fuel with their "Shifter" dragster. Then, in 1970, the pair split when Lee went funny car racing with a 'Cuda funny car. Abbott devoted his time to developing his Lenco racing transmission and of course his transmission business. In the early 1970s, Joe Lee's funny car became a test car for Abbott's Lenco transmission and other Abbott driveline parts and pieces. With testing came success for Abbott's Lenco transmission, as it became state of the art in racing transmissions for funny cars and top fuel dragsters.

The LA Hooker team of Beaver and Condit parted ways mid-1973. Gene Beaver took over the Mustang and put young Kenny Bernstein as the driver for the rest of 1973. But it was a very short tenure for Bernstein because, on July 13, 1973, Kenny's new ride ended badly at State Capitol Dragway in Baton Rouge, Louisiana. Bernstein was burned while driving the LA Hooker Mustang. He suffered second- and third-degree burns on his hands but did escape the rolling inferno as the LA Hooker burned to the ground.

Don Kirby (left) and Kenny Youngblood (right) took race car paint and design to a rolling art form in the 1970s. Working out of Kirby's Bellflower, California, shop, those two created masterpieces of rolling race car art. Neither was a novice to drag racing itself; Kirby had owned four funny cars from 1969 to 1971, and Youngblood owned and drove his Hemi-powered junior fuel dragster from 1968 to 1969 and was a silent partner in the Invader 'Cuda funny car.

The resident artist at Kirby's race car/funny car factory was Nat Quick. Nat was one of the most gifted artists to ever design, paint, and letter a race car. He was always ready to do a "quick" touch-up anywhere he was needed. He touched up the "Brand X" funny car in their pit area during the NHRA Springnationals in Dallas, Texas.

Jim Terry's Ford Mustang debuted in 1973 with Gordon Swearingen driving the purple-and-silver funny car. Terry had been a partner with Mike Thermos but went on his own in 1973 with this Plueger-built Mustang. This funny car was the first to run an 8-71 blower. Neil Leffler took his turn behind the wheel of Terry's Mustang at local events. On the other side are Gary Densham and his 'Cuda funny car for 1973. This was Densham's first funny car without a partner. Both cars were regulars at SoCal funny car events.

First there was the 1970 Prock and Howell "Warhorse" Ford Mustang funny car and then the 1972 Dave Mudrack Warhorse Ford Mustang funny car. Finally, in 1973, there was the Bishop, Tocco, and Buehl Warhorse Ford Mustang funny car. The 1973 Warhorse was raced by the ex-altered team and piloted by Roger Garten. Their Warhorse was built by M&S Welding in Azusa, California. The M&S crew was no strangers to building race cars; it built Dyno Don Nicholson's Ford Maverick pro stock.

Before Dale Armstrong became the iconic crew chief for Kenny Bernstein's Bud King funny car, he was a funny car shoe. Early on, he drove the Canuck Nova funny car and then Tom Sturm's two different funny cars, a Corvair and Challenger. Then, in 1973, he was driving the Hoover, Larsen, and Armstrong 'Cuda funny car. This car started out as an injected nitro-burning funny car that ran with the Southern California injected funny car circuit. A blower was added so the team could race in bigger-paying funny car shows. The trio disbanded at the end of 1973. Armstrong went on to race in NHRA's new Pro Comp eliminator with the Foust and Armstrong blown roadster and then the Veney and Armstrong dragster.

Doug Kruse was a metallurgist and an expert metal fabricator who built race car bodies. Kruse loved the sport of drag racing, with nitro burners being his favorites. During the late 1960s, Kruse promoted his own series of Professional Dragster Association (PDA) races in California. These races featured top fuel dragsters at first, and then funny cars were added to the show in the early 1970s. His events featured the absolute best cars from all over the United States, and the fans packed his PDA events. This is a promo photograph for his 1973 PDA event at OCIR. It featured PDA queen Barbara Roufs and Pete Everett's Lil Demon with driver Bob Pickett. Kruse liked the idea of a pretty girl with a race car to promote his races.

The OCIR Manufacturers Race was the pinnacle for funny car racers nationwide. It was the Super Bowl of funny car racing. Even though it was copied in the Midwest and on the East Coast, those never quite equaled the OCIR Manufacturers Race. Standing-room-only crowds were common at this funny car happening. Funny cars from all over the United States showed up for a piece of the large purse offered per round and, of course, the winner's purse. A strong showing could help with bookings for the entire season.

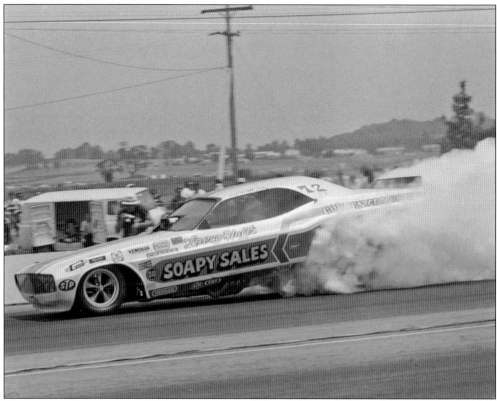

Remember the old saying "Looks can be deceiving?" This played out at the 1973 NHRA Springnationals in Columbus, Ohio. What looks like Larry Huff's Soapy Sales Challenger funny car is really the combination of two different teams. Under the Larry Huff Soapy Sales Challenger body is Rich Guasco's Pure Hell chassis and engine. The Huff/Guasco teaming along with Dave Beebe at the helm scored big in Ohio. The team took home funny car eliminator honors. This was a rare sighting of Beebe outside of SoCal, as he did not like to leave his family to race anywhere outside of California.

Ray Alley chose a Dodge Charger funny car for the 1973 racing season. This was Ray's eighth season of racing his lineup of Engine Masters funny cars. That line of cars included a 'Cuda, Duster, Cougar, Mustang, and now a Charger-bodied funny car—and, of course, Alley's Big Al, the 1934 Ford sedan-bodied, Allison airplane engine–powered exhibition race car in 1965. The first part of 1973 saw Kenny Bernstein drive the new Charger for Alley. Alley was busy with his Engine Masters business, so Bernstein toured the Charger for six months.

On April 21, 1974, drag racing lost one of its early SoCal funny car racers. Charlie "Opie" Wilson lost his life in an accident at a one-eighth-mile track in North Carolina. Wilson went off the end in his Firebird funny car and struck a group of oak trees. The result was that Wilson sustained a broken neck and died from his injuries at the young age of 52 years old.

After burning the original 'Cuda body off the Vels/Parnelli Jones funny car, the team replaced it with a Mustang body for 1974. The Flyin' Hawaiian Danny Ongais piloted the new/old Mustang-bodied funny car at Southern California events. At the 1974 March meet in Bakersfield, Ongais lived up to his nickname while racing Jim Dunn. Ongais soon left drag racing and entered the world of IndyCar racing.

One of the few African American funny car racers in SoCal was Clarence Bailey. Bailey raced funny cars through the 1970s. In 1971, Bailey drove his "King Cougar" funny car, and then, in 1974–1975, he raced his "King Boogaloo" Cougar-bodied funny car. He raced off and on until retiring in 1980 with a Mopar-bodied funny car. Bailey relied on Hemi power in all his funny cars. He was a regular fixture at Southern California funny car shows.

The only touring African American SoCal funny car racer was Barry "Machine Gun" Kelly and his Vega funny car. At New York National Speedway in 1974, Kelly had a big-time fire while driving his Vega against Tom Crevasse and the "Fireball" Vega. Kelly's Vega shed its body in the shutdown area and plowed into the rear of the Fireball Vega. Neither driver was hurt in the mating of the two funny cars. Kelly did receive burns from the fire and decided to call it a funny car career. The Fireball Vega was rebuilt, and Crevasse continued racing it in 1974.

June 1973 was not a good month for Roland Leong and the Revell's Hawaiian funny car crew. While on tour with the Revell's Hawaiian Charger funny car, they stopped to race at the US 30 raceway in Gary, Indiana. Leong and the crew drove down the road to the Holiday Inn in Gary, which was the base for touring funny cars in the Midwest. After checking in and parking the rig, the crew retired for the evening. The next morning, the crew discovered the entire rig was gone from the parking lot. Searching by local police and the Indiana Highway Patrol found Leong's tow truck and funny car chassis abandoned in Hobert, Indiana. The thieves were never caught.

For over 20 years, "TV" Tommy Ivo toured his top fuel dragsters across the United States, running 72 to almost 100 dates a year with his dragsters. With the surge in popularity of funny cars and the dwindling demand for touring top fuel dragsters, Ivo made the switch to a funny car. During the mid-1970s, Ivo toured a Mopar-bodied funny car, but it did not matter what Ivo raced—he was a true showman in either type of race car. When the costs of racing a funny car got crazy, Ivo went jet-dragster racing in the early 1980s. For him, it was all about pleasing his fan base and giving everyone a great show.

Do-it-yourself funny car owner/driver Jeff Courtie suffered a massive blower explosion and body launch at the 1974 NHRA Supernationals in Ontario, California. Nobody was injured, except Courtie's bank account. Courtie replaced the very hurt 'Cuda body with a Mustang II body and kept racing at local SoCal events. (Photograph by Mike Bagnod, courtesy of the Jamie Jackson collection.)

The Force brothers John and Louie purchased the former Jack Chrisman sidewinder-style Ford Mustang funny car from Roy Mehus. Mehus raced the car only a few times before selling it to the Force brothers. They repainted the car and replaced the SOHC Ford engine with a Chrysler Hemi engine and then named it the Nightstalker. One big problem with the car was it was chain driven. The brothers were banned from racing at Irwindale by starter Larry Sutton because the car would fling chain links all over the starting line when it ran. The Nightstalker was soon replaced with the former LA Hooker Vega funny car. The Force brothers bought the Vega from their uncle Gene Beaver. (Photograph by Rick Shute/Auto Imagery.)

A welcome sight at local funny car events in Southern California was Cindy Fullerton. Cindy was the daughter of funny car owner/driver Larry Fullerton. It was very brave of Larry to bring such a lovely daughter to the races. However, nobody messed with Cindy, and the funny car guys were very protective of her. She was a fixture in the Trojan Horse funny car pit area in the 1970s.

Funny car driver Bob Pickett did what most funny car
drivers did in the 1970s. He blended nitro and alcohol
with a hydrometer for the fuel tank on Pete Everett's
Lil Demon funny car. Besides mixing fuel, most
drivers of that era also packed their own parachutes.

In early Southern California funny car racing, not
many wives or girlfriends could be seen getting their
hands dirty. One of those "dirty girls" was Ann
Mineo, wife of Flash Mineo. Ann was the number-
one crewwoman for Mineo. She did everything from
washing parts to starting the car and backing the
car up. If necessary, she drove the funny car hauler
when the Mineos toured the United States.

One of the truly low-dollar funny car teams in Southern California was the father-and-son team of Eddie and Rodney Flournoy. This black father-and-son team purchased a well-used Jerry Ruth Mustang funny car in the mid-1970s. Together, with Eddie tuning and his teenage son Rodney driving, they made their mark in Southern California funny car racing. Because money was tight, the duo pretty much did everything themselves, and they did well enough to upgrade their race cars for almost 15-plus years of funny car racing.

Occasionally, there were days in Southern California funny car racing that were not very much fun. Funny car teams that toured had bookings to race five to seven times a week. This meant constant maintenance of the race car, as missing race dates was very costly. Racers could be found working anywhere and everywhere to keep their funny car running and making money.

The peak year for the popularity of funny cars in Southern California was 1972. However, there were dark days ahead, as in December 1972 Lions drag strip closed its doors forever. That left only two major tracks that held funny car shows on a regular basis. The oil embargo and gasoline shortages had OCIR and Irwindale management cut back their funny car events. The decline of funny car racing started in 1973 and continued through the 1980s.

# DISCOVER THOUSANDS OF LOCAL HISTORY BOOKS FEATURING MILLIONS OF VINTAGE IMAGES

Arcadia Publishing, the leading local history publisher in the United States, is committed to making history accessible and meaningful through publishing books that celebrate and preserve the heritage of America's people and places.

Find more books like this at
**www.arcadiapublishing.com**

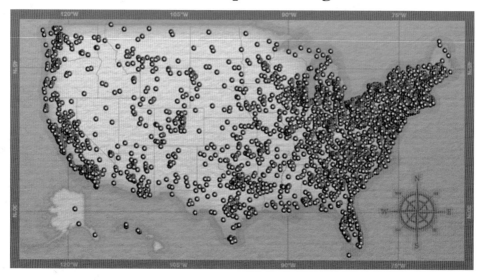

Search for your hometown history, your old stomping grounds, and even your favorite sports team.

Consistent with our mission to preserve history on a local level, this book was printed in South Carolina on American-made paper and manufactured entirely in the United States. Products carrying the accredited Forest Stewardship Council (FSC) label are printed on 100 percent FSC-certified paper.

MADE IN THE USA